TOMMY MELLO

ELEVATE

BUILD A BUSINESS
WHERE EVERYBODY WINS

MVHL

For permission requests, write to the publisher, addressed "Attention: Permissions Coordinator,"
carol@markvictorhansenlibrary.com

Quantity sales special discounts are available on quantity purchases by corporations, associations, and others. For details, contact the publisher at carol@markvictorhansenlibrary.com

Orders by U.S. trade bookstores and wholesalers.
Email: carol@markvictorhansenlibrary.com

Creative contribution by Veronica Deisler
Cover Design - Low & Joe Creative, Brea, CA 92821
Book Layout - DBree, StoneBear Design

Manufactured and printed in the United States of America distributed globally by markvictorhansenlibrary.com

New York | Los Angeles | London | Sydney

ISBN: 979-8-88581-085-2 Hardback
ISBN: 979-8-88581-086-9 Paperback
ISBN: 979-8-88581-087-6 eBook
ISBN: 979-8-88581-088-3 Audio book
Library of Congress Control Number: 2023902735

CONTENTS

Foreword
by Tom Howard

I MET TOMMY MELLO IN 2017 AT A CONFERENCE. I owned a small air conditioning company in Fresno, California. My company had just started doing plumbing as well. We were pushing about 10 million in annual revenue. We thought that we were on top of the world.

Tommy was doing a little less revenue at the time, but he was the one garage door company among scores of HVAC and plumbing shops. He stood out like a sore thumb. It wasn't just because of his chosen trade either. I quickly realized that he thought differently from all of us. I wouldn't realize just how different he really was until years later, but I knew that he definitely saw things on a whole new scale. While I was building my company like I built a tree house as a kid, Tommy was laying the foundation for a tree mansion that none of us thought possible.

I had met over a hundred different shop owners in my life up until that point. Some of them were quite large and some were small but all of them had plans. Most people had relatively conservative plans, but I had heard a few hot shots with big plans before. They usually would tell anyone who would listen about how big they were going to be.

Tommy had even bigger plans. I immediately discounted what he was saying and started to pass them off as pipe dreams, but the longer I listened to him, the more I realized he had truly thought of how he was going to pull off these ideas. He made me raise an eyebrow or two at that time, but even after hearing his plans, I still had a fair bit of skepticism. I still remember him talking to me at a party at that first conference. He said, "Tom, you gotta nail it before you scale it." He said it three or four times that night. Then he said, "I am going to get everything dialed in and then I am going to scale it after that. You watch." I kind of rolled my eyes. I thought "Yeah, Tommy, we are all trying to nail it. Let me know how that works out."

After leaving the conference, I kept in touch with Tommy and got to know him better over the years. I was shocked to see that he was actually executing on what he said he would do. People talk all the time. People have million dollar and billion-dollar ideas every day. Almost none of those people actually execute. He was not only executing on growing his company, but he was also executing on ideas that most of us didn't even dare to try. While most of us were looking for our next technician to help us grow, or maybe building a better incentive plan to attract new talent, Tommy was building a training center and buying an apartment complex to house all his new recruits during training. While most of us were increasing our marketing spend, Tommy was changing the way his company marketed altogether. He built partnerships with real estate agents, manufacturers, and even storm chasers. (I can tell you a whole story about that one.)

I didn't know it at the time, but even the conference where I initially met him was not intended for him. It was a ServiceTitan Conference called Dispatch. ServiceTitan, before that, hadn't even sold its product to garage door companies, and they had turned him down multiple times. Tommy ended up writing an email to the CEO, Ara Mahdessian, and convinced him to give the Garage Door industry a shot. Ara and Tommy both still have that email. Tommy knew software was one piece of his tree house, or tree mansion, that he needed. He took the ServiceTitan product and ran it hard. His staff learned the ins and outs of it, and he became one of the more successful shops on it. ServiceTitan had no choice but to put development dollars into features for the garage door industry and now has hundreds of garage door companies on the platform today.

Over the years, I would visit Tommy on multiple occasions. He would come stay at my place or I would go stay at his. By the way, most of the time when I went to his place, it was a two-bedroom apartment in the apartment complex that he owned. He started staying there as a short-term thing and then, before he knew it, years had gone by. He didn't seem to care. He was absolutely focused on building his "tree mansion."

Every time I went to visit him, and I do mean every time, we would stay up until at least 11pm talking about the business and Tommy's new ideas. I started to realize that no one was as excited about building their business as Tommy was. He would talk until I completely passed out. Then, at 7am we would start talking again. This is not an exaggeration.

There is another side to Tommy, though, that most people don't see unless they are close to him. Tommy mentions in this book that you need to find a way for everyone to win. That saying sounds like a cliché, but Tommy absolutely lives by it. He told me that he wanted to make a bunch of millionaires out of his employees. It's easy to get big and forget about all of those people that helped you get there. Tommy had planned on making sure that they got a cut from the very beginning. Most of them got a cut through performance pay, but he issued profit interest units to many of the original employees. He had given out so many that the president of the company had to call him on it at one point and make sure that he understood the significance of what he was doing. Of course, Tommy knew exactly what he was doing. The amount of money that Tommy was awarding to his employees, either through profit interest units or through their performance pay, was more than I ever could have dreamed of as a kid.

When I got married, I had $300 left in my bank account. My wife bought me socks for our first Christmas. It's all we could afford. I remember that around Valentine's Day, we had agreed that we wouldn't get each other anything. We went for a walk and saw what appeared to be a piece of trash in the grass. It was soaked from the sprinklers. We went to pick it up to throw it away and we found a certificate for a pound of See's Chocolate. We were elated. We literally ran to the See's store to see if they would still take it in its soaked condition. They did and we couldn't have been happier.

At some point, when we got a little more stable, I started saving up for knives for Christmas. My wife had one Cutco knife and she adored it. I would save up each year for one for Christmas. I would get the money to order one but usually didn't have the money in time to get it engraved. I really wanted them to be engraved but it wasn't in the cards most years.

Eventually, we got some extra cash, and we were able to make a set. Only four or five of the knives were engraved though. They were all white handled Cutco knives.

Ten years later, we were on our way out the door. My wife and I had gotten caught up with the hustle and bustle of life. By that time, we owned several companies generating over 50 million in total revenue. We had forgotten all about the struggles we went through as a young couple. Just before leaving the house, we got a package at the door. It was a silver box and we had to open it. It was from Tommy. It was a full set of white handled Cutco knives and every one of them was engraved with my name and my wife's name on them.

I had to stop. I was shocked. It changed my whole thought process. The hustle of life had caught up to me and Tommy forced me to slow down and think about where I had come from. Tommy continues to build his tree house or tree mansion or whatever you want to call it, but what good is a tree house without people to share it? I hope you will read this book and get a vision into many of the conversations and ideas I have been able to hear Tommy talk about over the years. Most important, I hope you will see Tommy for who he really is. If there is anyone you could learn from about maintaining an Elevate Mindset and developing skills in Leadership, Culture, Marketing, Recruiting and Systems—all while remembering your team—it's Tommy Mello.

Tom Howard owns multiple service companies in the central California area, including an HVAC and pest control company. After acquiring these service companies, Tom tripled their revenue or better in the first four years. In January 2020, Tom also joined Service Titan as a VP of Customer Experience.

Introduction: The Hundred Million Dollar Brainstorm

WHEN THE COVID-19 LOCKDOWN HIT and the business world turned upside down, I had a realization about success that changed everything for me and my team. The future was uncertain at my company, A1 Garage Door Service. One of my guys made a joke that I might be going back into the field. We didn't know there was going to be PPP (Paycheck Protection Program) money. We were stuck inside our homes. Customers were scared. And the thought of letting people in my team go broke my heart.

But then I went into the shop and discovered a line of people waiting outside my office. They all wanted to talk to me. Were they here to freak out? Or complain? Did they need something? Were they angry?

Before we can understand what they all said and why it matters, let's go back twelve years, to when my life and business were spiraling out of control. Back then I was a firefighter. Not literally, but it was my full-time job to put out work-related fires here at A1 Garage Door. I put in fourteen-hour days, seven days a week, without any vacations. I had four trucks, fifteen employees, and my mother was the acting secretary.

When I thought life couldn't possibly get any harder, two of my best employees confronted me on the same day about problems I couldn't solve. My number one tech asked for a raise, and my number two asked for a new truck. Retaining these employees was a high priority for me, but it would cost over $50,000 in the immediate short term to give the guys what they needed, and I didn't have that. This realization hit me in the chest like a sledgehammer. For a moment, I struggled to breathe. The guys genuinely deserved these things, and I couldn't afford them. I felt like a loser.

Before I could build a company full of winners, I had to accept the fact that the people on my team were struggling. My best employees were overworked, underpaid, and on the verge of leaving. Even worse, my business model didn't have the margin to reward my team for their hard work. This meant no matter how many hours we pulled, we were maxed out at $3 million.

That evening, I stared into my mirror for a long time. Except, instead of asking the self-pitying questions I normally asked, like: "Why don't they respect me?" or "How can I find employees who care?" I decided to ask something new. "What would it take for me to build a company where I can equip my employees for success?" I thought deeply about how that company would look and function. And I realized the business I was picturing in my imagination was different from the one I ran in real life.

I didn't sleep at all that night. For hours I lay awake, crunching numbers and churning through ideas in my head. How could I empower my employees? How could all the players on my team win big? The A1 dream was too small, I realized. What would be a dream that was big enough for everyone to get behind?

Arriving at the office when it was still dark, hours before everyone else, I mapped out my new vision on the whiteboard. At the top, I wrote the number $100,000,000. That's what I'd determined our revenue needed to be. Then I kept writing. I put down the goals, metrics, calculations, staffing plans, and logistics that would allow us to reach that number. I didn't stop until the board was full of words, arrows, boxes, calculations, sketches, and diagrams.

When my staff showed up for work the next morning, they found a new vision scrawled all over the walls. It was a vision for a company in which everyone could win. It was an important milestone. But having the idea is one thing. Building it in real life is another. That's what we spent the next twelve years doing. Then the year 2020 happened.

By the time COVID hit and the world went into lockdown we'd swollen to 150 employees and $75 million in revenue. The company I'd pictured twelve years earlier was closer to reality. But when the corona-virus took the world by storm, I wasn't sure what would become of A1. I braced myself for the worst.

When I arrived at work on the first day of lockdown to a line of employees outside my office, it was hard not to panic. If they were queuing up to complain, I didn't have answers. But I couldn't turn them away. So, I opened my door, stepped inside, and beckoned the first guy to follow. For the next three hours I met with every single person, and an incredible trend emerged.

Nobody was there to complain. In fact, everyone wanted to know what they could do to help the A1 family make it through this. They offered to take pay cuts and give up their accumulated vacation time so we could keep everyone employed. They said they would come in on weekends, organize virtual meetups, distribute sanitation supplies, and whatever else they could do to help the company stay alive. I was blown away by the kindness, thoughtfulness, and generosity.

"I want to be the best version of myself I can be," one guy said, nodding earnestly as he explained why he wanted to go without pay for a few weeks. "I'm going to be a leader in the company one day, Tommy. And leaders eat last, like you always say."

And that's when I had the epiphany that launched this book. Tears welled up in my eyes and I had to turn away to keep from losing it. The reason A1 was winning the game, I realized, was because we'd spent twelve years building structures to Elevate each and every member of our team.

After I worked through this process with my own company, and gained success, other entrepreneurs wanted to know how I was doing it. They frequently asked me to explain my business philosophy. So, I started a podcast to share my best tips. And I was invited to give talks and lead workshops for business owners. I've spent the better part of the last decade working with like-minded entrepreneurs to devise a comprehensive formula for building an Elevated business. Much of what you'll read in the pages that follow came through trial and error. But the formula eventually synthesized into a whole. Everything came together nicely into a concrete framework.

It has five pillars:

1. Leadership	2. Culture	3. Marketing	4. Recruiting	5. Systems

Implementing all five pillars of the Elevate philosophy in your own company may sound like work. What's in it for you? You'll get your life back. You can have vacations again. And weekends. Heck, you can even take celebratory trips to Cabo with your top employees (more on that later). In short, you will reach a point where you can finally run your business the way you want because the company is no longer controlling everything about your life. In fact, on some days you won't run the business at all, because it'll be running itself.

One of the best days of my life occurred when I wasn't in the office. I took a long weekend to relax, and didn't even check my phone. It felt great knowing my team had everything under control. And when I returned to work, I was greeted with a big surprise: on the day I was out, my sales team closed $512,000 in sales! At the time, that was the biggest day we'd ever had, by far.

This year, A1 Garage Door Service exceeded my $100 million target, and we're on track to do more than $150 million. In 2021 we brought in over $70 million in revenue. And we're still growing at seventy to eighty percent per year! We now have nearly 600 employees operating out of thirty-two locations spanning twenty states. And next year we're planning to grow revenue to the $300 million point. We have a winning formula, and the biggest winners are our employees.

While I was busy cracking the code on how to create an Elevated business, the job market shifted. Top companies used to have their pick of the best people. But now the top people have their pick of the best companies. Things have changed. We have more choice about where we work than ever before. And we are getting picky.

It's only going to get harder to attract and hire A-players to work for your company in the coming years. This trend isn't going away. Companies now have an additional set of pressures to contend with. Not only must we sell customers on why they should do business with us. We also must sell employees on why they should work for us too. Businesses that don't solve this new set of problems will go extinct.

But that won't be your fate.

To follow the Elevate way you must understand the five core pillars of a winning business. When you implement these concepts properly in your company, you can stop firefighting once and for all. You will never depend on a single person to run the show again. You can truly go on vacation and not worry about checking your calls or emails. Your company can double in size every year, no matter how the economy is doing. And, ultimately, you can build a business that sells for a large sum of money.

When your employees win, you win. That's the big secret. The question is: do you want to design a company where all your employees feel Elevated? Do you want a line of A-players waiting outside of your door, promising to do whatever it takes to make your company great? Do you want to build a premium brand that attracts the highest-quality customers and employees? If the answer is no, then shut this book right now, because nothing in here will be useful to you. Keep putting out fires and watching employees roll through your company like a revolving door. But if you want to share your wins with hundreds of people and grow your company by a magnitude bigger than your wildest dreams, then turn the page. Before you dive into the first pillar, take a quick look at your mentality. I want to introduce you to the Elevate Mindset.

Chapter 1
Embracing the Elevate Mindset

THE STORY MOST BUSINESS OWNERS TELL OURSELVES is that we build our businesses by working our asses off, but that's not true. Because if it were, you wouldn't be reading this book. The sad truth is working your ass off isn't enough by itself. A successful business isn't built by a founder working alone, but by grade-A employees working within a rock-solid structure. In the sports world, a winning team isn't built by a coach in isolation, but by a group of devoted athletes training in a fully equipped facility. In the Navy, a tightly run ship isn't built by a single commander, but by a crew of elite officers living together in a bulletproof submarine. In these environments, everyone knows the rules, understands their responsibilities, and feels the stakes—and so everyone performs. The problem is, however, that most companies aren't built like a top tier sports team or a tightly run warship.

In the world of business, most owners operate more like amateur athletes or soldiers, rather than seasoned coaches and commanders. Twelve years ago, I was no different. I worked my ass off putting out fires, talking to clients on the phone, driving the truck to take care of late-night emergencies, working weekends, skipping vacations, and leaning into my employees when they weren't up to par. We were making money, but we were miserable. And I knew our course was unsustainable.

I thought the problem was my employees. If they would only work harder, get more done, and take on some of the late-hour burdens, I'd have enough time to hire and train new people so we could grow the team. If only they took more initiative, I could look for ways to expand the company. It was a fantasy. The reality was some of my employees were stealing toilet paper from the office bathroom, and I was angry.

The thought crossed my mind that maybe I should fire everyone and hire new employees from scratch. It would be tough for a couple weeks, but maybe then I could get the company back on track. Somehow, though, I knew this wasn't the answer.

When a sports team gets relegated to a lower division, the first thing that usually happens is the coach gets fired. When a major fiasco happens in the military, the first person investigated is the commander in charge. But in the business world, owners are the last people questioned when their company is in the pit. And the reason for this is obvious: because they're the ones doing the questioning.

Business owners have a bad tendency to act like athletes and soldiers instead of coaches and commanders. The temptation to get in the action and put out fires is real. I get it. It feels good to solve problems and take care of imminent threats. You get a solid dopamine rush when you save the company from doom. You know that when you address a problem, it will get solved the right way. And maybe my employee will learn a lesson, you might think, optimistically. Jumping in and fixing the problem may buy your company one more day, but it doesn't help your team grow. You need to allow your employees to fail and put out their own fires. It's the only way they will learn. Just make sure that they know what they're accountable for first. If everyone is accountable, then no one is accountable.

If you want to turn the business around, you must accept the truth: you are not the answer to your company's problems. Your employees are. You can't do everything that's needed all by yourself to plug the gaps and fix the business. It's going to take a team of A-players to get everything done. Your employees aren't the problem; they are the solution.

Most of the time when your employees fail it's because you set them up to fail. So, to turn your business around, change how you treat employees. You can't blame them for your problems anymore. Instead, show them how to win and equip them for victory. Give them a world class athletic facility or an impenetrable warship.

What's wild is that once you start to Elevate your current employees, you can also Elevate your recruiting, so that every new person you hire continues to raise the bar of excellence within your company. And you can Elevate your own leadership to the next level, too. At the same time, this allows you to Elevate your pricing, revenue, and margins.

Missed Opportunities

Allan was stuck. For almost a decade his small HVAC company had been stalled out. He tried everything he could think of to increase profits, but nothing worked. It was a company he'd owned for thirty years, and he was running out of time, money, and ideas. With his three children all in college, Allan's savings had vaporized. His accountant called one day to warn him he'd officially gone into debt. If something didn't change soon, he was going to lose the family home. Allan had to find a way to turn his business around.

From the outside, Allan looked happy and successful. His business did about $5 million, with a staff of eight technicians. There were ads for his company on yard signs, radio commercials, and newspaper ads. He had a loving wife and great kids, and he often posted pictures on social media of his family taking exotic vacations around the world.

Behind the scenes, however, a different story played out. Over the previous decade, his marketing budget had ballooned. Meanwhile, revenue barely held steady. Each year Allan grew increasingly frantic as he watched his profits shrink. He worked around the clock, on weekends and holidays, and was constantly exhausted. Allan felt like his problems were crushing him from all sides, making it hard to breathe. At one point he was so desperate that he sent emails to a dozen local investors and business owners, asking if they wanted to buy his company. He never heard back.

Allan was beat down, but he wasn't ready to give up. He calculated he could afford to keep his company open four more months. He vowed that, during that time, he would do everything he could to fix the business. Then, if it still wasn't profitable, he would have no choice but to close down.

The problem, Allan thought, was that he'd hired the wrong people. If his techs cared more, tried harder, and improved quicker—like Allan did—the business would be thriving. His employees massively underperformed. They complained when Allan micromanaged them, but when he gave them more freedom, they got sloppy and made careless mistakes. No matter what he did, nothing got through. Sometimes he fantasized about firing them all and starting over.

To turn things around, Allan reasoned he needed more structure and better ways of monitoring his employees. So, he made a list of rules and implemented penalties for breaking them. Not surprisingly, employees hated this system and rebelled against the rules. They called Allan "The Warden." Embarrassed, he hastily dissolved the rules and rolled back the punishments. But the nickname stuck.

Next, Allan took the opposite approach, creating a system of rewards and incentives to motivate employees to try harder. His techs could win bonuses by hitting benchmarks either individually or as a team. Except, the crew all balked at the benchmarks. They said they were already doing the best they could, and what he wanted was impossible.

In response, Allan vowed to spend more time training his people. He dedicated an hour every morning to giving workshops on how to be a better technician. He was up well into the night most days, preparing for his lesson the following morning. Unfortunately, Allan wasn't a great teacher. His employees complained the workshops were a waste of time.

Allan was at the end of the road. He was frustrated, sleep deprived, and emotionally beat. Nothing had worked and his business was still bleeding money. But why? Hadn't he tried all the conventional wisdom for turning a business around? He'd built structure, offered incentives, and took responsibility for training. He was fulfilling the duties of a business owner, wasn't he? Did he have bad luck?

The four months were nearly up, and Allan realized the game was over. It was time to quit. He took the afternoon off to go for a long walk and clear his head. This has been quite a journey, he thought to himself, but it's over now.

That's when he got a call that changed his life. One of those emails he sent out about selling his company had made its way to a group of investors who buy HVAC businesses. They wanted to meet with him right away.

The investors moved quickly, and within two weeks Allan sold his company for $6 million. It was a miracle! His finances were secure, and he was finally able to relax. He slept in as late as he wanted, ate whatever he felt like, and even watched ESPN on weekdays. His old worries were someone else's problems now. Allan had to admit life was good.

While Allan might have been relieved to cash out and move on, he missed a huge opportunity. Over the following year, the investors who purchased his company implemented a series of small but significant changes, and the results were astounding. First, they shifted hiring practices and changed how they marketed to and recruited new talent into the company. Next, they created a tight and focused team culture, where people had fun at work but were hungry to win. Finally, they built systems to assist employees and teach them how to do everything the company required.

Under this new leadership style, profits soared. The company grew quickly. Within a year, revenue was over $9 million. Then, a year later, it was $22 million. Allan's happily-ever-after fairy tale ending is, in reality, a what-could-have-been warning story. He had been sitting on a gold mine, if only he could have figured out how to dig deeper. Allan failed to Elevate his employees, and it cost him a big opportunity.

What did Allan do wrong? It boils down to one thing: mindset.

When Allan took four months to try to turn the business around, his mindset was: save the company. The problem with this mindset is that it is self-centered. Allan was the sole owner of the company. So, his mindset was more along the lines of save myself. Unsurprisingly, his employees never got on board with this mission. Why would they be excited about working to help Allan win?

Twelve years ago, I found myself in a similar place as Allan. I knew I needed to make radical changes at my company, or it was Game Over. But before I went about implementing any new policies, I took one important step that made all the difference. I took the time to consider how big my company's goals had to be for everyone to win.

When business owners operate from a save-the-company mindset, there can only be one winner, and that is the business owner. Even if employees do put in long hours and keep the company afloat, what do they get? A pat on the back? Maybe a raise? Or maybe they quit.

When I decided to turn my company around, I set a revenue target of $100 million dollars, and I created an equity incentive program to get the members of my team all rowing in the same direction. I knew if A1 made that much money, everyone in the company would win. And a company where everyone wins is a company I wanted to build. But how?

With a tangible number on my whiteboard, I mapped out everything that had to change for A1 to become a $100 million company. How many technicians would we need? What skills should they have? What about their tools? Uniforms? Training? How much should our best techs be paid? What kind of pricing model would make this all work? How many sales would we be making? For the most part, I followed my gut. I didn't get everything right at first, but as I put these ideas into play, my employees did stop stealing my toilet paper. Once I changed my attitude, their attitudes changed as well.

While setting a goal to achieve a revenue target of $100 million was great, I knew there was another step. My focus also needed to be on our profits. Businesses often brag about their revenue, but few of them talk about their profits. I knew that mindset had to change. "Revenue is vanity, profit is sanity," In other words, growing revenue without growing profits is useless. Once the cost of doing business is paid for, it's your profits that will determine your success and future growth.

If you want a winning mindset on your team, do these two things:

1. Find a way for everyone to win
2. Assume full responsibility for any and all losses

When you can get these two power moves working together, magic happens. This is the Elevate Mindset. Let's look at both of these ideas in closer detail.

Find a Way for Everyone to Win

Human beings are born to compete, but we need something to fight for. We're naturally driven to win. It's in our DNA to collaborate in small groups. But we need a reason to struggle. People can endure horrific conditions if we have a strong enough motivation. This is even true in horrific situations like the Holocaust, as Viktor Frankl pointed out in his classic book, *Man's Search for Meaning*. The most important thing he learned in living through World War II in a Nazi concentration camp was having a deep reason to survive.

We all need a reason for doing what we do, and this is especially true for work. We spend the bulk of our waking hours every day working. And for many of us, our jobs aren't sources of passion. That's a huge problem.

There are many theories about what's wrong with the modern workplace and how to get employees more motivated, but what it all boils down to is that people need opportunities to win. Humans will work hard on something for a long time to win. But when a situation feels hopeless, we give up and check out.

In many businesses, employees can feel like parts in a machine, performing simple repetitive tasks someone told them to do. While that might be the most efficient way to produce an F-150 every fifty-two seconds, it's not inspiring. When your job is to put on a few screws or solder a few wires or install a windshield in the same way all day, it's easy to lose touch with the deeper purpose of your work. Everything becomes about logistics and details, and you can get pulled away from the emotional core of what you're working on.

As a leader, it's your job to show everyone how their tasks help the business win. The worst thing you can ever say to someone as a manager is, "Because I told you so." If an employee asks why they are doing something, that means they don't understand the reason behind their task. They are disconnected from how what they are doing helps the team win.

I once noticed someone from my team kept putting off a program I wanted done for an accreditation. When I talked to her about it, she said, "I don't understand why we're doing this." So, I realized it was my fault for not explaining it. She wasn't motivated because I lazily assigned the task to her without communicating how it would help us win. That's why she kept putting it off. The secret I didn't know yet was "what's in it for her?" I hadn't used a proper delegation process.

"This will get us accredited," I said, looking her directly in the eyes, "so the government can start sending discharged vets to us. And the military will sponsor them for $10,000 per person to get training on how to succeed in the home services industry. So, as soon as we get this done it opens up a huge new stream of students into our training programs."

She got it done that same day.

When the pandemic hit and my employees lined up outside my office ready to work, I knew they were driven by more than generosity. They wanted the company to survive because there are tangible ways for them all to win here at A1. They are connected to the company's success and because of that, when it needed help, they were ready to step in.

So, why don't you have a line of A-players waiting outside your door, asking how they can help your company win? Make it a win for them, too. That's the Elevate Mindset. Think about how to make sure everyone is winning.

Maybe there is still something more your company must become to attract the top people in your industry. Maybe your competitors offer better pay, newer vans, more vacation, or a more laid-back work environment. It's likely that if your business was a place where you made it easier for people to win, you would have more interest from high-quality applicants. Also, it's important to never rest on your laurels. In fact, at A1 we recently redesigned our vision and mission to be even more employee centric.

Darren Hardy is a *New York Times* best-selling author, a keynote speaker, an advisor, and former publisher of *SUCCESS* magazine, Although he was a man at the top of his game, he had difficulty when it came to dating, He wasn't sure what he wanted in a woman, and he wrote a list of a hundred things that made a perfect woman. Then it hit him. The perfect woman would never look twice at him. And he wasn't sure he deserved her anyway. So, he created a new list of a hundred things he could do to attract a good woman to him. Then he set out to become the man who would be worthy of that woman.

I'm no expert on dating but, like Darren, I've spent time thinking about what we must become in business to attract the right people. One of the most important things we need is ways for our employees to win. People love to win. Everybody wants promotions, raises, bonuses, and recognition. We all want to feel like we are making moves in our careers and getting ahead. And we prefer companies that provide those opportunities.

One of the most basic examples of giving people opportunities to win comes down to how you pay your employees. At my company we have a big equity incentive program. Anyone who wants can become an owner. We can all get some skin in the game. That's something any company can set up. Talk to a lawyer about it.

By sharing equity with employees, you can make them feel like partners with you in building the company. Employees who own stock in the company become invested in its success. It gives them a stake in the outcome. It also puts them on the same page as the other shareholders. Employees with a vested interest in the business are more likely to stick around and feel motivated to do their best. Another advantage is that it's a way to hire good people when you can't meet their pay requests, and to give existing employees a raise without spending more money. The more invested people feel in your mission, the better. Because when others are invested in your mission, everyone can win together.

Take Responsibility for Any and All Losses

Once you're in the mindset of looking for ways everybody at your company can win, it's time to shift how you think about losing. While most business owners generally consider it to be the employee's fault when they don't hit their targets, the responsibility lies with the business. Adopting the mentality that failure is never the employee's fault encourages you to respond to losses by doubling down on support, training, and resources, rather than with punishment.

An example of taking responsibility for failures happened recently at my company. I realized we had a problem with how we onboard new Customer Service Representatives (CSRs). Our policy was to pay CSRs either $13.50 per hour or their bonus, whichever was higher. And the bonus was almost always higher. The policy encouraged hard work because it prevented them from earning a bonus unless they performed. However, this created a problem during the training period.

During training, there weren't any opportunities to earn a bonus. Everyone only made $13.50 per hour. So, no matter how promising the recruits, they only made the bare minimum when they first joined the company. In other words, there weren't any ways for them to win.

"Do you mean to tell me," I said to my team, "that this company I love is paying a dirt-poor salary to our people during their first weeks here?"

"Well," my CSR manager told me, "we don't want to incentivize them to hang around and do the bare minimum."

"If that's what's happening," I said, "then we're hiring the wrong people. But I believe we're hiring the right people, so let's pay them like they're the right people!"

See, the Elevate philosophy is that if we have recruits slacking off and doing the bare minimum during training, that's our fault. We've failed to set everything up properly as a company if we're seeing that behavior. It's not that we somehow got unlucky, and this was a bad batch of recruits. We interviewed and hired these people. So, if they suck, is that something we can blame on them? No! It's 100 percent our fault.

We'll see different behavior from our next group of new hires if we do something differently next time. Also, as our systems improve throughout the company, we're constantly going to get better at hiring the right people and training them. This problem will disappear if we fix the issues upstream in our recruiting process that are causing us to hire employees who don't care.

As business owners, it's our job to take ownership for everything, especially the losses. But don't go around beating yourself up and apologizing for everything that goes wrong at the company. That sounds sad.

Taking responsibility can be empowering. See, I can't control my employees. I can provide them with rules and regulations, but I can't guarantee anyone will follow my guidelines. The only thing I have control over is how I act. So, if my company's losses are an employee problem there isn't much I can do. But if I'm the problem, that's something I can work on.

When your people fail, it's on you to Elevate them to success.

Putting it Together

One business owner named Al Levi saw firsthand the magic of what can happen when these two ingredients of the Elevate Mindset come together perfectly. For years, Al tried unsuccessfully to scale his family plumbing, heating, and cooling and electrical company. Al and his brother Richie ran a business they took over from their father in Long Island. They had about twenty-five techs and did around $17 million in revenue. The brothers worked around the clock and were always last in the office every night, often not leaving until 3 am

With an established company and an experienced team, it seemed like the men should be able to take time off, enjoy their lives, and step away from the business—but they were held hostage. It was the same story Al remembered from his childhood, with his father getting pulled into the office on weekends, evenings, and holidays.

As a kid, Al worked in the business every summer and winter vacation. In college, when he had a week off for spring break, his father celebrated by letting Al drive a different delivery truck than normal for the week. The business had been running Al's life ever since he could remember, and he was sick of it.

As the brothers looked at the business their father had built, they saw one problem after another. Employees were paid full price for mediocre performance. Sometimes management wouldn't learn someone had quit until customers called to complain a tech never showed up. Employees stopped coming into work, and Al found their keys hanging in the locker room. The brothers argued constantly.

One day Al and Richie sat in a seminar, listening to a speaker talk about the industry.

"Technicians are aging," the speaker said, nodding soberly. "Soon the average age will be over fifty years." The brothers looked at each other. This was a chilling thought. They didn't want to be running around chasing emergencies when they were fifty years old.

They weren't sure what to do next. Al and Richie were overworked, underpaid, and stressed out from managing their business. Was it supposed to be this hard? Al decided the answer was no. He walked into the office one day and spoke up about his concerns to Richie, saying, "I don't know about you, but I'm tired of feeling like a hostage at our own company."

Richie agreed. "So, what are you going to do about it?" he asked.

"I don't know right now," Al said, "but I'm going to figure it out."

The brothers needed to somehow trade their squad of mediocre employees who they didn't trust for an amazing team of superstars who could help them get to the next level. But how?

First, Al and his brother developed a clear organizational chart or "org chart", which delineated the chain of command and outlined the career path for employees. Now anyone could see at a glance that there was room to grow at the company. The chart even spelled out which skills employees had to master at each level to move up to the next one. And the brothers worked hard to develop materials to help new hires learn the skills referenced on the org chart.

With this move, Al created an obvious set of systems to give employees ways to win. He found A-players responded to this and he soon hired a big team of great people. But not everyone performed similarly well after getting started. In fact, some struggled. Now that he was confident he was hiring excellent people, he needed better systems to support his people and Elevate them to win the game.

Next, Al built out a series of modules for a curriculum that trained his recruits to become experts in their crafts. He developed systems for monitoring performance and rewarding rock stars. The company decided to take responsibility for making sure employees got results, rather than hoping they did well.

It was work to make all these changes to the company. Many times during the months it took to implement these ideas, the brothers got into fights about whether it was even worth the effort. In the end, though, they got it done. And when they did the results were immediate—the company exploded.

Today, Al coaches other business owners on how to implement the system he and his brother discovered all those years ago. His book, *The 7 Power Contractor*, has helped thousands of entrepreneurs scale their businesses to the next level. In fact, I'm one of those entrepreneurs. I met Al six years ago, when I had a small business with thirty employees, and his teachings were foundational to my success. His words at a seminar I attended were my first glimpse at my idea for the Elevate Mindset.

Over the years I've experimented with what Al taught me, making updates and improvements along the way, simplifying things, and looking for better ways to communicate the principles. I've taught these ideas to hundreds of entrepreneurs and seen stories like Al's and mine play out far too often to count.

In analyzing the differences between companies full of A-players and ones stacked with losers, I've noticed five major trends. And they parallel the ideas Al taught me back when I was first starting out. These are the secrets to attracting and retaining a team of top-performing employees to work for you. They are the five core pillars of an Elevated Company. This book explores them all.

THE FIRST PILLAR

For the first pillar, you'll see that employees respond best when we flip the standard model of leadership on its head. Instead of micromanaging our employees, we can Elevate them. And when we do, they will thrive. But what does Elevated leadership look like? How is it done? How can we train other leaders within our organization? I'll show you two key changes to make in your leadership style and I'll give you a simple scorecard you can use in your company to improve leadership across the board.

THE SECOND PILLAR

During the second pillar, you'll learn to create a winning culture, the bedrock of the Elevate way. A killer culture is a magnet that attracts A-players to work for your company. It feeds into all other pillars. I used to think culture was stupid, but then I discovered a simple strategy for consciously creating a winning culture in any company, and I was hooked. It's not abstract; it's science. There are studies on what businesses can do to develop the right culture. Over the years I have experimented with an arsenal of tools for doing that, and I'll share them with you.

THE THIRD PILLAR

Once your culture is under control, you'll learn to market your company as a great place to work. That's the third pillar. If you want a line of A-players waiting outside your door, those people have to know you exist. And they need some reason for thinking your company looks like a better place to work than others. So, how can you spread the word? Entrepreneurs commonly use marketing to attract the right customers and position the product as appealing. But why not also use marketing to attract the right employees and position the company as an amazing team to join? I'll show you some secret strategies that will blow your mind.

THE FOURTH PILLAR

Recruiting is the fourth pillar. Once those floods of applicants come in, how do you sort through the deluge? How can you determine which people are the true A-players? Unfortunately, now that your marketing is making your company look so good, everyone wants a job with you. And they will all try to convince you they can get you massive results if you give them a chance. But every entrepreneur has been burned by employees who seemed great at first and then turned into nightmares.

These mistakes are costly and unnecessary. There are effective ways to screen out the prime candidates, and I've discovered some powerful tactics. I'll show you how we do it here at A1, and how you can apply the same ideas to your business.

With those four pillars in place, the final pillar you'll need is a set of systems to keep everything working without your direct attention. An Elevated company has detailed systems for hiring, onboarding, training, rewarding, disciplining, promoting, firing, and honoring employees, among many other things. As you hire new A-players, you need a solid set of systems to drop them into. This is their training facility. It's their submarine. These systems are your way of equipping your people for success. In my experience, most business owners don't even have a fraction of the systems needed to be truly competitive in today's economy. I'll show you how to assess your needs and plug the gaps.

This book will reveal how you can develop systems to Elevate your employees and give them ways to win. As you read, you'll construct your state-of-the-art training complex and write your playbook. You'll build your bulletproof submarine and create your Code of Conduct. And anytime something goes wrong in the company from now on, you can look to the systems for places to fix the issues, not to your employees.

THAT'S THE ELEVATE MINDSET. STUDY IT. LEARN IT. LIVE IT.

Go On a Winning Streak

There's an odd trend in sports that when a star player gets injured during an important game, the rest of the team tends to step up and go on a winning streak. As long as the injured player didn't play an integral position (like quarterback or goalkeeper), the rest of the team usually rebounds with lethal force. Like a wounded tiger backed against the wall, such teams generally come out flying when play resumes after the injury. Whether the phenomenon is emotional, adrenal, mental, or all of the above, it happens frequently.

Perhaps the most visual example occurred in a National Hockey League match between the San Jose Sharks and the Las Vegas Golden

Knights. It happened when the Sharks lost their captain, Joe Pavelski, in the third period of a Game 7 playoff match. It was 2019 and the Sharks were down 3-0 in an elimination game to their rival Knights. With ten minutes in the game, Captain Pavelski (aka "Big Joe") got tangled up with a Golden Knights player, slipped, and cracked his head on the ice.

The home crowd went silent as blood spilled from the back of Big Joe's head and he was helped off the ice. The Golden Knights player was given a controversial game misconduct penalty (a high price for what looked like an accident). That was when veteran Sharks star Joe Thornton (aka "Jumbo Joe") looked at his team with those red-hot eyes and massive salt-n-pepper beard and said, "Go score four goals."

The situation the Sharks faced that night on the ice is almost identical to the scenarios small businesses often find themselves in. The hockey players were down in points, and people were counting them out. The deck was stacked against them. Entrepreneurs are often trying to make it through these types of high-stakes situations. We're trying to land an impossibly big new client or to get our product mentioned in the national media or to finish a huge proposal on a crazy turnaround. The Sharks players were skating on thin ice as play resumed after the penalty, like many business owners do every single day.

With ten minutes left in the game, down 3-0, and now down their captain, it would have been reasonable to expect the Sharks to lose. Even with a five-minute major power-play, scoring four goals in a hockey game is an obnoxiously hard task. The Sharks could have put in a hard final ten minutes, maybe scored a goal or two, still lost, and the fans would have applauded and said, "Dang, nice try. Thanks for the show. Maybe next year."

But that's not what happened.

The following play happened immediately after the match resumed, and it took six seconds: the Sharks won the face-off, made one pass, took a shot, it was blocked, they collected the rebound, passed it to Assistant Captain Logan Couture, and Couture buried a shot into the top-left corner of the goal. Then Couture turned, looked at his bench, held up a finger, and shouted, "That's one!"

Fifty seconds later the Sharks entered the attacking zone and dropped a pass to defenseman Eric Karlsson, who took a slap shot from the blue line. It deflected off the stick of Sharks centerman Tomáš Hertl, who was standing right where Big Joe normally stands on the attack. The puck flew past the Vegas goaltender and into the net. The second goal.

The home crowd went nuts. Their team was now one goal away from tying what was a hopeless game only seconds before. Suddenly, hope buzzed in the air. The stadium was electrified with anticipation. And when the puck dropped, every single fan was on the edge of their seat.

Vegas, realizing the threat of a lost lead, stepped up their game. They forced San Jose out of their zone and held the line for as long as they could. But the Sharks were relentless. With eighty-one seconds left on their power-play they gained zone control, passed the puck to a wide- open Couture, and watched as he snapped a shot point-perfect into the net.

The place erupted. Couture stretched out his arms and soaked in the glory of the moment. The impossible had happened. When he got to the bench the team mobbed him. They were back in the game. They were even. Now, they could win.

The crowd was still celebrating when youngster Kevin Labanc skated into the offensive zone with the puck. Few people may have noticed, but Labanc had an assist on all three of the previous Sharks goals. In the spur of the moment, though, he faked a pass, rushed toward the net, and with two players and a goalie blocking his view, he fired a seeing-eye shot into the lower corner of the goal.

Hockey was never so loud. The people in the stands went crazy as Labanc celebrated with his team. If Couture was mobbed, Labanc was smothered. The team dog-piled him over the boards. After all, they had accomplished Jumbo Joe's high ask of them. They had scored four goals.

The Sharks went on to beat Las Vegas 5-4 in overtime, and all without their captain. This feat could not have happened on any team, though. When Big Joe left the ice, the bookkeepers gave the Sharks a 2.1 percent chance of winning the game. It took a team of grade-A players stepping up at the right time and for the right reason to win. There was no single superstar carrying the squad. Everyone had to pitch in to secure the victory. And when the final buzzer sounded, the whole team got to celebrate. Even Big Joe back in the locker room screamed his head off.

Of course, no team wants to be in the situation the Sharks were in when Big Joe was carried off the ice, but every team would like to know they have what it takes to accomplish what the Sharks did in the aftermath. The same can be said for your business. You don't want to be in a situation where you need four times the work to be done and you're down one of your best employees. But wouldn't it be nice to know your team could handle that pressure if the situation did arise?

It's easy to look at the Sharks victory after losing Big Joe as a story about ten minutes of incredible hockey. And it certainly was an amazing bit of play. But it was also more than that. What made those ten minutes possible was the previous ten years that the owners and coaching staff of the Sharks spent building systems for recruiting, training, and managing a winning team.

Let's not forget that behind the Sharks dogpile on the bench there were coaches and managers working for years behind the scenes. Before the Sharks could celebrate their epic win, they had to go through a carefully designed system that was engineered and built from the ground up to prepare them for success. The same is true for your employees.

In the chapters that follow, you'll learn about the five pillars your company must have to Elevate your employees so everyone can win. It's time to start your own winning streak.

Al Levi's Best Tips

Since he played such an important role in my own mindset shift all those years ago, I wanted to include some advice in the book directly from Al Levi himself. We sat down and had a great conversation.

"Whoever owns the techs," he told me, "owns the world. My father used to tell me that. But I had no idea what it meant!"

Al said he worked in his father's business for years before he finally had the revelation that led him to understand the profound wisdom of this simple phrase. Instead of giving him a management position, Al's dad forced him to drive a truck. Finally, fed up that he hadn't been promoted, Al asked his father when he could move up in the company.

"You are never going to get out of the truck," said Al's dad, "until you figure out how to get other people into it."

At that moment, Al realized his mindset was wrong. He wouldn't be promoted to a leadership role until he became a great leader. He wasn't going to get a free ride. If he wanted to move up, he had to step up. The only thing holding him back was himself. That was when his mindset shifted.

Eventually, he was promoted as he came to adopt the Elevate Mindset, finding ways for everyone to win and taking responsibility for every failure.

Years later, Al had a great client who said that how a company orients an employee during the first two weeks dictates the relationship. At first, Al thought that was crazy. But he soon realized the guy was right. Hiring works best when the business gets new people paired up with mentors right away, teaches them the systems, and helps them get some quick wins. When this happens, employees are more likely to stick around.

Good businesses sell people a career, Al says, not a job. And then they keep selling it. Employees must see a path for their future, from Day One. What will it look like to go from apprentice to junior tech, to senior tech, to field supervisor? What are the milestones? How long will it take? And you can't tell them once, during orientation, and then drop it. People will forget how it all works. So, Al recommends frequently reminding them. Show everybody the org chart often. Point out where they are, and reiterate what it will take to move up to the next level. When Al did that in his business, he was able to stop the brain drain of top talent leaving the company and going out on their own.

Another big thing Al did to stop the brain drain was creating a program for senior techs to run their own businesses from within his, without all the hassle of managing a big company for themselves. At A1 we can offer plenty of upward mobility because we are growing so fast, and people like that. We are opening locations and constantly need new branch managers. Think about how you can provide room for growth, even as your employees climb to the top rungs of your ladder. Can you add new rungs beyond that? What's next?

Offer people chances to keep winning as they grow. If you can't, it might be time to expand your vision.

One of the biggest shifts in mindset Al went through in his career managing people, he says, was switching his philosophy on hiring. Initially, he recruited people with skills and hoped they were hard-working. Later, he switched to recruiting hard workers and taking responsibility for teaching them the skills. That's when his business took off.

Taking responsibility for training your employees to be winners isn't a one-time commitment, it's ongoing. Al spent time and money building a massive training center to teach his people everything they needed to know. Then he set to work writing detailed manuals for every employee. But, once those manuals were done, he realized he needed to go back and change the training center. So, he rebuilt it. And he's gone back to redo it many times since. He now sees maintaining his training center as a constant process.

Adopting the Elevate Mindset helps you retain people better, Al says. When you commit to helping them improve themselves, employees will be loyal. They are getting recruited all the time. Remind them that if other companies weren't willing to invest in training them before, why would that change now? Of course, not everyone will stay. But people like to grow. Support them in that and they will stick around.

Chapter 2
The First Pillar: Leadership

SOMEONE IS GOING TO LEAD YOUR COMPANY through a big transition period to implement the pillars from this book. And if you're the one reading, that someone is you. Are you up to the task? Unfortunately, many people have flawed perceptions about leadership, which cause them to treat their employees in problematic ways. That can leave you stalled on the side of the road before you even get going.

Typically, we think of leadership as a relationship in which one person reports to another on an org chart. The leader has higher status, is often more senior, may be more experienced or talented, and makes more money. The leader is up above, and the employee is down below. Information flows from the leader to the subordinate, not the other way around. This typical view of leadership is problematic because it suggests the way to gain more power as a leader is to raise yourself up high, and to keep the people you lead down low.

On the other hand, there is another view of leadership as well. Instead of leading from up above and hoping people follow orders, we can lead from down below, supporting and Elevating our employees. We can stand beneath and raise them up. A good coach doesn't hold himself above you, he sits on the sidelines while you play, guiding you and cheering you on.

Running this process to Elevate our people requires two main things: Leadership Systems, and passion. When we implement both ingredients successfully, our employees will naturally view us as strong and wise leaders. But it's rare to see managers or business owners who possess a healthy balance of these traits. Usually, one comes more easily than the other. We are either systematic leaders or passionate leaders. But Elevating our teams requires both. How do we achieve the right balance?

Brian Davenport has experienced the two dynamics of balanced leadership firsthand in his work to develop systems for teaching and measuring the effectiveness of leaders. But there was a time when he struggled in his career, and it was affecting his whole life. He was feeling fed up with his stressful work in the garage door industry. He didn't agree ethically with the business practices of his company, or the things his manager asked him to do. But he felt stuck. He had a sour taste in his mouth about the garage business.

Some of Brian's close friends were about to move to Jacksonville, Florida, and they invited him and his fiancée to come with them and start a new life there. But, as the pressure was mounting to make a decision, he ran into an old colleague, Kevin, who was now working at a different garage door company. Kevin said his new job was amazing.

"We're doing things in this industry that nobody else is doing," Kevin said, with passion, and Brian thought he saw a tear come to the guy's eyes. "Our CEO has an amazing vision. Are you looking for a new job?" Kevin asked.

"Well," Brian thought for a moment. "Yes, I am."

"Awesome," Kevin smiled. "I'll set up a meeting with you and our CEO. He's this enthusiastic dude named Tommy Mello. The company is called A1 Garage Door Service."

Later that evening, I gave Brian a call and we ended up chatting for quite some time. He impressed me with his insights into the garage door industry. He knew how to manage A-players and get them to run in the same direction. Also, his experience working at a franchise company would help me enter new markets. I wanted him to come work at A1. We set up a meeting for the next day.

During our meeting, Brian admitted he was leaving his current job. His options, he said, were either this job with A1, or moving to Florida with his friends.

"Well then," I said, "it's my goal to convince you to stay in Phoenix."

At the time, I had recently attended a workshop with Al Levi where he talked about building a scorecard that you could use to measure how well each employee performed. Al said this level of assessment was the key to good leadership, and I thought Brian could be the right guy to help me build that system out at A1. He seemed to have a good mind for organization, structure, and process.

Today, Brian is a leader in our organization. He helps train our managers and he develops systems for improving leadership within A1 Garage Door. One of the biggest things he oversees is our wildly successful Scorecard program.

Thanks to Brian and our incredible team, we've discovered the magic of what can happen when every employee has specific KPIs (Key Performance Indicators) and performance pay for hitting those numbers. Leadership becomes easier once you put appropriate Leadership Systems in place. Now your job becomes Elevating your people and lifting them up to help them hit their goals, earn more money, and move higher in the company. In this world, you meet with them regularly to review their progress and talk about how they can hit their target numbers. At A1, we define the OKRs (Objectives and Key Results) for each employee and have a Dream Manager who's responsible for helping them achieve that. Implementing these ideas has been instrumental to our success and our ability to delegate work and manage employees effectively.

I hear so many small business owners complaining about their workers, but what does that reveal about their leadership abilities? They say things like "If I don't do it myself it won't get done right" or "Well, I told him how to do it, so if he couldn't figure it out that's not my fault" or "It's not rocket science" or "Everyone around me is a certified idiot." But these types of statements shift blame away from ourselves and onto our employees. That's not productive.

Putting employees down is the opposite of Elevating them. Lift people up. Help them see beyond their potential. Give employees chances to make mistakes because that's how people learn. If we blame them and shame them for every error, soon they will be afraid to do anything wrong.

If your people aren't doing something right, is it possible you didn't set them up for success? Did you give them an exact process to follow? Do you have a way of holding them accountable? Most people can figure things out; they don't need you to treat them like they're stupid. They need the right tools and instruction, then they can take it from there. If your people are having trouble, check the tools and instructions you gave them.

Everyone in my industry seems to be talking lately about how they need great people to work for them, but nobody is talking about how they wish they were better leaders. Isn't it the same problem though? Great people come from top coaches and mentors. Everyone is looking for lightning in a bottle, hoping to hire employees who already know everything without training or even onboarding. But that's not realistic.

Great leaders have awesome teams, but leadership is hard. Mike Tyson said something interesting to me recently about leadership.

"I can't coach, Tommy," he said. "Coaches are cut from a different cloth, man."

It's true. Have you ever noticed you don't see many superstar athletes go on to be amazing general managers and coaches? You'd think all great coaches would be former top players, but that's almost never the case. It's because coaches are cut from a different cloth, like Mike Tyson said. The traits that make someone a good leader aren't necessarily the same as the traits of a good team member.

People tell me all the time they have trouble with their employees. Managers complain that millennials don't want to work hard. I can't tell you how many times I've heard passionate conversations about how hard it is to find "good people these days." But I don't buy that.

Millennials aren't prima donnas. They want to be appreciated for their efforts, like any human being. They want to know there is a ladder to move up in the business. They want clear direction on what it will take for them to progress up the org chart and move forward in their careers and in their lives. Make employees feel appreciated and give them ways to win. That works regardless of what generation they come from.

Good leaders Elevate people, consistently giving them slightly higher responsibilities that allow them to learn and grow. These leaders delegate, they don't micromanage or take over at the last minute and do the work themselves. They push people to ever greater heights and they also push themselves, too.

One trap many leaders fall into is spending too much time focusing on the lowest performers in the group. However, bringing up the bottom is a losing strategy. It's easy to focus on the worst people because they stand out. These employees drag down the team. Surely something needs to be done with them. Intuitively it makes sense that if the worst guys could get three times better, the overall performance of the group would jump significantly. However, this is an illusion. Even if the worst people get three times better, they still often aren't on the same level as the best people.

As an example, my top guy currently does $3 million per year in sales, and my worst one does about $400k. That means if my worst guy gets three times as good, he'll do an extra $800k next year. But if my best guy even improves by fifty percent, he'll do an additional $1.5 million. So, the return on investment from putting energy into your best people is higher than focusing on the bottom. Imagine what would happen if leaders put more energy into mentoring their hits, not trying to salvage their flops.

However, even amongst your hits there will be a variety of people and work ethics you'll have to deal with. Part of your responsibility as a leader is to find out what works best for each individual on the team. Each employee might have a different, preferred way to brainstorm, communicate, and receive feedback. You want to pick up on those differences and facilitate everyone.

No matter who you're working with, there are two universal ingredients to Elevated Leadership: systems and passion. Let's explore these one at a time in detail. Then we'll see how they fit together.

Leadership Systems

Whenever you're in a leadership role and giving out instructions, tell people what's in it for them. At the end of the day, that's all any of us care about. We want to take actions that benefit us. In the work world the main benefits we can get are promotions and raises. Good leaders often build systems to link specific actions they want employees to take with outcomes those employees care about. Building and fine-tuning these systems is one of the big ways that sets apart exceptional leaders from mediocre ones.

Good leaders use a certain type of system, called a Leadership System. These are structures designed to reward employees who meet and exceed expectations. Having them in place is a way of promising employees that if they perform well, they will be compensated.

These systems also give employees a feeling of "Oh crap" and that's by design as well. We're monitoring them closely. They can't screw around on the job and expect to be promoted. When they see how detailed our systems are, I want them to feel scared.

There's a book called *The Coaching Effect,* by Bill Eckstrom and Sarah Wirth, which says high-performing managers "create feelings of healthy discomfort" for their teams. I couldn't agree more. Something I say all the time is "We're the best we've ever been, but the worst we'll ever be." Another variation I also like to say is "BYB: Better Your Best." It's awesome to celebrate the progress everyone is making, and a good leader should hand out some praise every day. But you want to push people out of their comfort zone. After all, that's how we improve. Good work—let's keep moving.

Leadership Systems are helpful because they tell people what you want them to do. There is an old saying in business that what gets measured gets managed. This is a big part of the philosophy behind Leadership Systems.

The way this works is you give each of your people scorecards, so they know how they are doing in the important areas. Nobody's score-card should have more than five items on it. You need to keep these focused, or they quickly become confusing and overwhelming.

The items on this scorecard are an employee's prime objectives. Review their numbers with them frequently so they can see how they are doing. They should know where they stand.

When you have one-on-one meetings with people you can give them the floor to share what's going on. They will naturally go through their scorecard and talk about how they stack up and what to do differently to hit their goals. And you can sit back and let them do the dirty talk instead of having to lead it yourself. They should report to you on a regular basis about their progress, so if they aren't reaching their goals, they owe you an explanation.

You can also tie the scorecard goals to the existing personal goals of the employee. This enhances motivation and makes these conversations feel more collaborative, rather than disciplinary. You get to the point where you can offer them some help, like "I know you didn't hit your goals toward that home you're so excited to buy for your family. Why don't you let me mentor you twice a week and bring up your numbers?"

When you're leading someone who keeps making mistakes or missing targets, what can you do? In general, you likely have one of two main problems: either they don't understand what to do, or they don't want to do it. So, either they need training or motivation. Come in and say, "Listen, you've got to want this as bad as I want it for you. I want you to reach your goals. But do you want it for yourself?"

The basic idea is if employees hit their goals in certain areas, they can earn bonuses. However, don't incentivize every goal on the scorecard directly. Some can be assumed as part of the job. For instance, I'm not going to pay my technicians more for driving well. That's assumed. If they drive poorly, I've got to fire them. There are certain areas where you want to pay for performance, and others where that doesn't make sense.

At A1, for example, nobody cares whether the company hits $150 million at the end of the year or not, because that doesn't make a difference for each individual employee. But if the company promised everyone a bonus for hitting that number, suddenly there's an incentive for every single person in the organization. That's one example. The idea is that it's up to me as the leader to find ways to get people inspired about our group goals. And I can be as creative as I want.

What are your biggest goals as a company this year? What's in it for your employees if you manage to hit those goals? Human beings all operate from the principle of "What's In It For Me?" So, if you want your team to care about helping the company hit its goals, show your employees how you can help them accomplish their goals in return.

A big problem with many leaders when it comes to goal setting is inconsistency. A good leader should be unwavering, in dogged pursuit of a certain goal. Good leaders offer firm and consistent objectives for the team to latch onto.

When people from outside of my company hear our daily team calls, they think I'm crazy for focusing so closely on the same five things every single morning. They tell me I should switch it up sometimes. But that's missing the point. I want to repeat the same five things. I want people to have those ideas drilled into their heads. That's leadership. Good managers understand the importance of consistency.

What's the goal in your industry that everyone hopes to one day achieve in their careers? Cops want to get out of the field. Professors want to get tenure. Lawyers want to make partner or get appointed as judges. Every industry seems to have some milestone to strive for. That gives us all something to aspire to, which is important because we will have to put in some hard years to get there.

If you create an opportunity where people can work their butts off now, and one day get out of the field, or somehow get promoted to a more secure career, they will do it. In fact, this is the kind of structure effective leaders create. Once you have it in place, your job becomes Elevating people and helping them achieve their own personal goals by succeeding within your structures. That's where passion comes in, the second ingredient of balanced leadership.

You Need Passion Too!

Once we have the right types of systems and scorecards in place, the second quality good leaders have is passion. They pump people up to work hard and excel within the systems. Implementing leadership systems is like building a racetrack and agreeing to host a big event.

Once that's done, we motivate our driver to get out there and win the race.

I have a call every morning with my technicians to teach and inspire them. This morning I mentioned that I hung out with Larry Fitzgerald yesterday. He's a world-renowned receiver who played for the Cardinals. He said, "Tommy, I've caught over 1,400 balls during games. But you want to know what my little secret is? I've caught over 14,000 in practice." Wow, what a great piece of wisdom. When he said that, it lifted me up. So, I passed it along to Elevate my team. My mission on these calls is to pump my people up as much as possible. I think about it all day, so I'm prepared with something motivational to say. "If you want to be number one," I said, "it's pure grit, determination, and showing up to prepare. Have you caught 14,000 balls?"

I tell my technicians, "I'll give you everything to help you win, if you're willing to ask." If someone wants it badly enough, there's no reason they can't succeed here. I'll pay people good money to do ride-alongs for them to learn how more experienced techs do their appointments. We can role play different scenarios as much as they want at our training center. The idea is to have high standards and strict codes of excellence, but then give everyone more than enough support and guidance to succeed.

People will work hard to move toward a brighter future if you can paint that picture for them. Everybody wants to know there is a ladder up. They want to progress in their careers, move up, and earn more money. That's what everyone wants. So, sell people a plan to move up and get the life they dream of. Then coach them to work through the plan you developed.

I introduced myself to ten new call center service reps today during their training and said, hello.

"You all couldn't be at a better place," I smiled and waved. "I want to tell you how excited I am because we're growing, adding new positions, and creating a ladder for success. There are ten of you starting today, twelve more in two weeks, and more after that. I'm going to need a lot more supervisors coming up, and managers from there. And the sky's the limit, because at a fast-growing company new positions are created as people increasingly specialize."

With the passion of leadership comes the tendency to give plenty of praise. Great leaders are the type of people who love to Elevate others. But the paradox of great leadership is that it's not helpful to give too much praise. Find a way to be enthusiastic but not overly complimentary.

One manager told me an elaborate story he was clearly proud of. He said he heard a podcast about the power of praise, so he brings a roll of pennies into the office each day. And every time he gives a compliment, he moves one from the right pocket to the left. So, by the end of the day he tries to give fifty compliments out.

"Nice idea," I said. "But give me ten nickels instead of fifty pennies. That's way too many compliments."

Not to be a jerk, of course, but there is a proper balance of praise to feedback. It doesn't help people learn if you pump them up all the time with compliments so you can move over your pennies. What if an employee comes by your office at the end of the day for advice and he needs a stern warning, but you are low on pennies for the day? You'll end up heaping compliments on him when you should have scolded him.

Striking the right balance of praise is one of the biggest challenges for me as a leader. Often with my employees there's this dynamic where it feels like I'm a dad, and they want me to be proud of them. They want to know they are doing good, and everything is ok, and I care about them. Sometimes they look up at me with these hopeful faces. They all want feedback. They want to know what I think. They want me to say, "Hey, you've worked hard. I'm proud of you."

Advanced Leadership Tactics

Even when you have great systems and passion there are still things you can do to take your leadership skills to the next level. Let's look at vulnerability, empathy, and indirect leadership. These tactics are like the double black diamonds of management; ridiculously challenging, but absolutely worth the effort.

The first idea to consider here is vulnerability. Recently I took some time to think about my faults, and write them down (and, man, I've got faults). I tried to look at myself from the perspective of another person. He doesn't listen most of the time, he's high energy, he can lose focus, there are times when you work three weeks on something, and he only wants the three-minute synopsis.

Imagine if you were dating someone, and on the first date they said, "Hey, listen. Here are my downfalls: Sometimes, I'm hard to communicate with. There are times when you'll think I'm not paying attention. Actually, I do have a little bit of ADHD (ok, maybe a lot). There are times when I need you to help me find the solutions. I need you to point out where my time management is poor because that's something I struggle with. The best way to communicate with me is face-to-face, but I prefer text over voice calls."

If someone told you that on the first date, they might seem crazy. But then you could never come back later and say you didn't know how nuts they were. You knew everything upfront, fair and square. They gave you plenty of warning about their quirks.

Vulnerability is effective in leadership too, not only dating. When you share your faults and struggles it humanizes you and helps your people relate to you as a complex human being. And it helps your team to recognize you aren't perfect so they can cut you some slack.

Another tactic I sometimes fall back on during difficult challenges is an indirect leadership approach. It's when you get other influential people to help you out at important times. Instead of suggesting something yourself, sometimes you can call someone who you know an employee admires and ask them to plant a seed with the employee for you. Then when the time is right the idea will pop into their head. Be careful with this, because if the target finds out you asked other people to talk with them in your place, they can feel manipulated. It's good to be open about the fact that you spoke with the influential person about the issue.

Brian Davenport's Best Leadership Tips

Since Brian Davenport has been running our efforts with scorecards and Leadership Systems here at A1, I spoke with him about the biggest lessons he's learned over the years. He mentioned some interesting points I hadn't considered discussing in the book, so I wanted to include some of the highlights here for you. I should also credit Al Levi, whom Brian and I both learned this from in the first place. We brought him in as a consultant to help us build our scorecards.

Brian, Al, Adam Cronenberg, and I sat together in a room for two days straight hashing out what would appear on our scorecards. Al explained that everything should flow out of our revenue goals. Since we wanted to make $65 million in revenue, we then developed six high level KPIs to get there. Then we brought those bigger goals to our department heads, to break them down into smaller, more specific sub-goals. Then, the team managers took those sub-goals and figured out what each individual team member must do to keep the company on track to hit its revenue projections. Brian then used those numbers from the team managers to build out individual scorecards for every employee at A1.

When designing scorecards, differentiate between items that are critical versus merely important. This allows you to measure the right things in the right ways. The important distinction is about whether or not a certain activity advances your company toward its deepest goal. Usually, the deepest goal of a business is tied to revenue. For us this year it was to hit $150 million dollars. So, anything that helps us do that was critical. Other things might be important, but aren't on the same level of priority.

During one meeting when Brian and his team were designing scorecards, someone brought up perfect on-time employee attendance as something the cards could target. But the team ultimately ruled that out as a goal because, while it might be nice, it doesn't directly help us do $150 million. While attendance is important, it isn't critical.

You know something is a critical metric, Brian says, when you can calculate what it needs to be to hit your revenue goals. For example, you can determine how many calls per day your salespeople must take, and what their booking rate has to be, to close enough business. At A1, our scorecard for CSRs (Customer Service Representatives) measures all kinds of things, like vocal tonality, call quality, booking rate, call length, and the speed with which the phone was answered. For these we can calculate where each CSR needs to be as an individual so we can hit our goals as a company.

You have to treat your company like an assembly line. Everyone should become a specialist. You don't want a CSR doing the work of a dispatcher. If everybody is accountable for everything, then nobody is accountable for anything.

It's also important in a business that everyone's individual goals are aligned and in harmony with each other, Brian pointed out. And the scorecard system allows for that. Think about a fleet of battleships in the open ocean. They travel in a tight formation, all heading in the same direction. Companies are like that too. If everyone focuses on the same big goal, you can arrive at the destination on time together. And if one of the ships strays off course, the entire fleet can help bring it back into formation and continue their heading together.

Once scorecards are in place for every employee, says Brian, we meet with them daily as a team and weekly and monthly as individuals, to look at their performance and see how it measures up to their benchmarks. If you wait until the end of the month to see where your people are with KPIs, then you're already behind by a month. The same is true if you don't check back until the end of the quarter. As leaders, we want to look at where our people are now. What happened last week? Are we on track this week? Where can we adjust things to stay on schedule?

This approach is a huge difference from what most companies do. In a typical corporation, employees might have an annual review to look at their performance and compensation. By that point the manager is a full year behind. Additionally, they often don't have specific performance metrics to evaluate people by. So, they are a year behind with their data and they're flying blindfolded.

Another great thing about the scorecard system, Brian adds, is that it becomes obvious when someone is falling behind. It's obvious to them, their manager, and everyone on the team. This is especially true when the scorecard is paired with frequent one-on-one conversations. As a leader, the scorecard gives you a clear, organized, and detailed way to give feedback to your team about their performance.

Another thing you can do is take someone who struggles with one specific area of the scorecard and pair them up with someone who is crushing it there. This way they can learn from each other.

Brian doesn't remember ever having to fire an employee for scorecard performance. He says when people see that they are consistently failing to hit their numbers, they often come to him and ask for help. They want to know what they can do to bring their performance up. He's even had people resign and say, "I can't do what you're asking me to do. I love the company and everyone here, but this position is not suited for me, so I'll go find something else." It's great when people realize organically that they aren't a good fit, rather than having to be fired.

Scorecards can be emotional. When you review these with your employees, you're often telling them they aren't hitting their goals, and that's hard to hear. Brian says he's seen tough guys break down and cry during these conversations. They are deep talks that can unleash a flood of emotions. But this doesn't happen on its own. After all, the scorecard is only a piece of paper at the end of the day. What matters is what you do with it, and how you use it to have these critical talks.

Chapter 3
The Second Pillar: Culture

IF YOU THOUGHT ABOUT SKIPPING THIS CHAPTER, I GET IT. I used to make fun of entrepreneurs who worried about the culture at their companies. Business is about hard math, right? Not something soft like people's feelings. I was convinced economic success followed a simple formula: profit equals more money coming in each month than going out. And culture doesn't fit anywhere into that basic equation. So, I could ignore culture and still win big in business. To be frank, any talk about corporate culture always sounded like confetti-talk to me.

But what I've realized is this. It's not the topic of culture itself that's for show. The problem is the way 99.9 percent of people discuss it. Building a winning culture isn't about holding hands, doing "trust falls," or crying in each other's arms while talking about inclusivity. It's about hiring people who vibe well together and doing whatever it takes to make your company an amazing place to work. It's creating an atmosphere where all people feel uplifted and supported every day by the community at your workplace—not weighed down, made fun of, or stressed out.

The most obvious benefit of a winning culture is enhanced productivity. When a business has a positive culture, everyone gets more done. People don't waste time on petty interpersonal issues. Like the weather, a negative culture can blanket a team overnight in ten feet of snow, and freeze all progress to a standstill. It's easy for everyone to be happy, positive, and productive when the culture is sunny with clear skies. But when a storm rolls in everyone runs for cover. When you can improve the culture at your workplace, everyone will feel great, collaborate better, and get more done.

There's another big benefit to having the right culture at your business, too, and it's even more important than the productivity boost. You see, a dynamite culture creates a magnet of happiness that pulls A-level new employees into your orbit automatically. In the next pillar I'll show you how to market your company to potential employees as an awesome place to work. But that's only possible if you have a great culture to sell. Then, in Pillar 4, I'll explain how you can specifically recruit new employees who will fit well into the culture you're building.

Though it's possible to excel at recruiting without having a great culture, it's quite difficult. And even if you do pull it off, things tend to break down shortly thereafter. When new employees are thrown into a crumby culture, the situation can quickly turn toxic. Before long, people leave in a huff. So, even if you could be strong at recruiting without building a phenomenal culture, why would you want to? It wouldn't be stable.

Culture Problems

Would you rather work for a company where your job is guaranteed to be safe next year or one where you must keep your numbers up to maintain your spot? There are some businesses where people who have been working there for a long time are "safe" and nobody would ever fire them. A prime example is academia, where professors receive tenure and become nearly impossible to fire. But is that a good thing?

I believe any culture where people can rest on their laurels is suboptimal. Fear makes us great performers. Nobody at my company has a job next year for sure. Not even me! If I don't hit my numbers, the board of directors can decide to bring in a different CEO. And that would be fair. It doesn't scare me. I like feeling the pressure to keep my performance up.

It's toxic whenever anyone gets a crown on their head no one can take off.

Another thing that's toxic is a culture of mediocrity. Think about the bright-eyed new kid who gets hired and is working her ass off, then someone says, "Hey, you're working so hard over there. Pace yourself. Don't make us look bad."

Mediocrity is toxic, and our company culture should be designed to stamp it out. We want a culture where it's not OK to be average. Counter-intuitively, the worst employee is a good employee because you'll fire them right away. And a great employee is awesome to have, of course. We all want more A-players. But what about an employee who is just . . . kinda . . . pretty good? These people are the worst. You don't fire them because they aren't bad enough. But they never become superstars. So, they hang around, sometimes for decades! Establish a culture where it's not OK to be average. Flush out these mediocre employees. If you do this right, your people will police each other, and you won't have to be the referee.

When a company has a bad culture, it leads to bad meetings and a general feeling that people are wasting their time every day at work. I used to hate the word "culture" many years ago, but then I woke up and realized I was the problem. Yes, we needed a better culture to attract more competitive talent. We needed it so people would stick around longer and refer their friends to come work for us.

You might think you're special and your product is changing the world, so you don't need culture. But there are a million places to work. Now, more than ever, employees have options. So, why choose you? What makes your company special? Whatever it is, that's your culture. Capitalize on it better.

Modern workers don't like a culture where employees are pressured to sacrifice their health and pull long hours to hit short-term performance deadlines. Today's employees value their health and wellness. They want to work somewhere that supports them in caring for themselves, physically, spiritually, and emotionally. In one recent survey from the Workplace Trend Report, eighty-seven percent of employees reported wishing their company offered healthy workspace benefits, like wellness rooms, standing desks, healthy lunch foods, and ergonomic seating.

The issue of healthy workplace benefits comes back to Elevating your employees by equipping them to win. In isolation, a chair might not be a big deal. But when you imagine yourself sitting on that chair all day long, for hours on end, and years to come, the chair feels more important. For me, personally, a chair needs to be comfortable if I'm going to sit in it all day. I also like having the option to stand while I work, too, at least for part of the time.

I've gone through so many chairs, but they start squeaking after a couple months. The problem is that I bounce around all the time. They can't handle my insane nervous energy. I'm constantly going a hundred and fifty miles per hour, and it freaks the chairs out. But finally, we found one that works for me, and I love this chair. It's made a huge difference in my day. And I've made sure to provide good quality chairs for all of my employees. Put in the effort to find everyone the right chair, even if it takes time. Your employees will appreciate you for it.

I know a guy who is a consultant, and when he came in to work with one company, he could immediately see people were resistant to him. He needed to find some way to win the employees over and prove he was on their side. As a first move he bought everyone new chairs. And that won him respect. People saw he cared about their comfort, and they were grateful. Then he slowly implemented other strategic changes from there. Ultimately, he turned things around at that company.

Seriously, chairs matter.

Recognition can shape the culture at a company also. As the leader, be careful who you recognize, for what, and how. People notice who gets publicly praised. Humans are hard-wired to wonder how we can earn the same respect as others. So don't take this lightly. Don't randomly dish out compliments whenever you feel like it. Develop systems for recognizing people when they reach certain thresholds in their recruiting prowess.

Realizing the importance of recognition has inspired me to work harder at it myself. I'm now working on developing a recognition software to systematize this process in my own company. It's another important way to keep employees motivated.

It also helps every business owner to get into the mindset of thinking about yourself like a media company. If you have employees, put out a publication for them regularly to share updates and make them feel like part of the team. This is an important tool for consistently reinforcing company culture.

In addition to a regular newsletter here at A1 we're active on social media too. We get pictures and videos of people during training, and tag everyone when we post those on various networks. When we take the crew bowling for a fun company bonding experience, we bring our trusty social media people to film everything and take pictures. But before we had any marketing team, I filmed events myself with my smartphone. The key is to blow a curated stream of propaganda out to the company and beyond, through every possible channel.

This is where Culture connects into the next pillar: Marketing.

You can amplify your efforts by firing everything you do out to social media or an email newsletter. It reminds employees about your efforts and reinforces their role within your company. For instance, we cook breakfast and lunch for the guys. Whenever I can, I'll come down in an apron and help out, and we'll feed a huge meal to the company. We have fun with it. And, of course, we film that and post about it on social media, so people who weren't there can find out about it, and those who came can relive it again.

I also reach out to many of my employees personally on their birthdays and anniversaries to congratulate them. And I make a big deal about it when people get promoted and hit milestones in their careers. While sending out mass communications to your company is vital, it doesn't take the place of individualized messaging directly from you to them. Employees feel it when they receive personal attention from the founder, CEO, or their manager. As I sit here writing this, I'm working on better systems to recognize my employees.

You can think about your company culture as like three concentric circles, one inside of the other, inside of the third. The middle circle is the core attribute of your culture. Then the central and outer circles are the secondary and tertiary aspects of your culture.

Consider what the three main attributes are for your culture, or for the culture you wish to create. Try and get these down to one word each. What's the biggest, most important thing in your company's culture? What about the second most important attribute? And the third?

For me and A1 Garage Door Service its:

1. Competitive

2. Collaborative

3. Fun

Let's break these down and I'll show you how they apply in more depth here at A1. This way you can get a better idea of what your own cultural values might be, and how to make sure those things are reflected in the daily operations.

First, We are Competitive

Winning is at the heart of my company's culture. But not winning at the expense of others. We want to win together. We want to elevate each other to greater heights. I am looking for a certain attitude from my people, where they should be aggressive but not mean.

Henry Ford built a competitive culture in his organization, and it fueled massive levels of growth and productivity. That's what I want to do here at A1 also. One day, Ford famously strolled through the factory at the end of the day shift and asked how many Model Ts the men had completed. When they told him, he nodded and chalked a big number 7 in the middle of the factory floor.

When the guys got there for the night shift, they asked what the number meant, and someone told them the boss wrote it down because that's how many Model Ts the day shift got done. The night shift usually got four cars done. But somehow that night they did eight.

The next morning, when the guys from the day crew arrived, the 7 had been smudged out and replaced by a big number 8. That day, they managed to finish nine cars. Then the night guys did ten. The factory made it all the way up to fourteen cars in a single shift this way, when previously seven had been the record. With competition they were able to do twice as much as they ever had before.

The competitive spirit at the heart of A1 isn't about being mean to others, it's about never giving up, because you don't want to let others down. I don't care if I lose, but I'm going to try ten times harder than anyone else. That's the culture we've created at my company. You don't love losing. It doesn't feel good. But at the end of the day, what matters is that you worked insanely hard. If you do that every time, you'll win big in the long run.

A group of entrepreneurs and I were hanging out with Mike Tyson at an event in Los Angeles, and he said some wise things. Honestly, sometimes you have to think hard to understand what the heck Mike is talking about, but it's worth the effort. His work ethic is unparalleled, and we can all learn something from him.

"Too many people are talking about determination these days," he spat. His booming voice easily cut through the bustling sounds of the hotel floor, and the crowds of tourists seemed to melt away in front of him as the burly boxing champion led us toward the buffet.

"I don't buy any of that," he continued. "Consistency beats determination all day long. If you show up consistently and practice, you can't help but get better."

He's right. That's the story of the Tortoise and the Hare. Put one foot in front of the other and never stop. Winning isn't about doing everything all at once. It's about making the right decisions consistently over a long period of time. As Bill Gates would say, "Most people overestimate what they can do in one year and underestimate what they can do in ten years."

I love to hire people who were athletes in college or who played in the top-tier high school orchestra, sang in the choir, or won first place at the state science fair. These employees are used to being regimented and they know how to compete. They understand that if they figure out the right habits, and do those things consistently for an extended period of time, victory is all but assured.

Determination is difficult to measure, but consistency is easy to see. Either someone is taking the proper actions on a regular basis, or they aren't. So, Mike Tyson has a valid point.

If someone knows how to compete, then they already understand the importance of consistency. I want these people on my team. If you've never had any competition in your life, you won't last long in the A1 culture. And that's intentional. We only want A-players. Our culture is specific.

The culture of your company is reflected everywhere. Even foundational decisions like how to pay people reflect the culture. Personally, I don't like anything other than incentive pay. It creates a culture of high performance and internal competition. That's what I want.

Another thing I like about incentive pay is that it aligns interests between employees and management. There's a weird thing that happens in some companies, where it feels like workers and executives are on different teams. It's a negative kind of competition, when people are more focused on winning in small groups than winning overall as a company.

With performance-based pay, on the other hand, my executives and I want to pay our people as much as possible. Because that means everyone is making more money. We all win together. Now, suddenly, we're motivated to help our people win, so we can all win. This was one of the biggest shifts I made that impacted the culture at our company. When pay is tied to performance, A-players make the most money. That perfectly lines up with our values as a company, and that's how we should pay.

Performance pay is for winners. Losers don't make money with it. Imagine, I gave you the choice between an $80,000 base salary with the potential for a $5,000 bonus, or a $50,000 base salary with the ability to earn a $100,000 bonus. Which option would you choose? Do you want the higher ceiling, or the higher floor? This harmless hypothetical is a great way to test whether someone is a top performer. An A-player would want the higher ceiling because he's confident he'll hit it.

I try to pay all employees in a way that motivates them to compete fiercely. That's what started the conversation over how much to pay our CSRs. We paid our CSR managers either a few dollars above minimum wage per hour, or their Bonus. They don't get both. Good CSRs easily make $25 per hour. But bad ones make the minimum. The idea behind this system is that I want to pay people so if they under perform, they're not going to make good money. Whereas an A-player will kill it.

The caveat is that sometimes you develop a policy, thinking it aligns with your cultural values, only to learn later on it doesn't. In fact, that's what happened with our CSR pay. For a while, things were great. But eventually we noticed some A-players were turned off by the fact they could only make $13.50 during training, and there was no room for bonuses. We had to recognize they were right. We weren't paying people like A-players. In that regard, the policy was not in alignment with our values.

Competitiveness is one of those human traits that's difficult to go back and put in place if the individual didn't have the basic software installed successfully during early childhood. That's why I like to hire people who played in the orchestra, did karate, did model car racing, or somehow learned to compete while they were growing up. I need people who know what it takes to win. And you can't teach that to someone who didn't have it instilled from an early age. Becoming an A-player requires a burning desire to beat the other team.

One thing I've implemented to help maintain a culture of excellence and competition within my company is something called the Pinnacle Club. This is reserved for only my top performers, who do over a million dollars in sales. Last year we had fifteen of them, including their significant others. Everyone who makes it into the club gets a flashy red Masters jacket, a full year of bragging rights, and two tickets for an all-expenses-paid five-star trip to Cabo for a week, where they can party on the beach while drinking bottomless Corona and tequila shots. I come out for the trip, and everyone brings their spouses with them. It's a great time.

I also bring my social media team to the Pinnacle Club trip where they can follow us around the whole time and film everything. And we post the videos and promote them to everyone at A1. The trip reinforces our values of winning and being the best. And it gives all the techs in the company something to aspire to, this mythical number of doing a million dollars in sales.

The trip is a huge motivator within the company, and it also serves as marketing to potential new employees too. Everyone who sees our recruiting ads that week and comes across our social media channels will see a stream of updates from the trip to Cabo. And they'll see the top people in the company having a blast and being rewarded. And if they resonate with our values, they will apply.

If you don't have the budget to take trips to Cabo, that doesn't mean you can't put together this type of event. Even a tiny company can buy pizzas and post pictures on social media of the team having a good time. You're killing two birds with one stone. People love the opportunity to hang out and have fun, and also don't mind sharing these on their social media.

What I love about the Pinnacle Club is that there is no limit to how many people can win. There's not a first, second, and third place. If every single tech in my company does over a million dollars in sales next year, we'll all be going to Cabo together. The more, the merrier. That's perfectly in line with the type of competition we value here at A1 Garage Door Service.

We don't only dangle the carrot of Cabo to motivate our people here, we carry a big stick too. And we're not afraid to use it. From the first day of training, we make it obvious that we are not afraid to send people home if they demonstrate they aren't a good fit for our culture. The thing at A1 is people get their work done. If you don't, you look like a fool. Everyone notices and it's obvious.

Another key to a high-performing culture is pride. I know it might be one of the Seven Deadly Sins, but I find pride to be quite helpful for success in business. You want your people to be proud of what they do and where they work.

I noticed huge bumps in pride whenever I bought updated trucks. I swear, those guys stood six inches taller when they rode around on some new wheels. I realized those spotless trucks made my employees feel more valuable as human beings than the beat-up old ones. So, I decided to keep our techs driving brand new trucks. This policy, admittedly, is quite expensive. But it adds to our culture of being the best. And it makes our guys feel like a million bucks as they ride around the city. That's huge.

In fact, I've heard from experienced techs who move around to many different home service companies that the single most important question to ask about a company to determine whether it's a positive place to work is "Do the drivers have new trucks?" Word on the street is this one question tells you everything about how a business treats their people. If they don't have new vehicles, they don't have a great CRM, and they're not spending much on marketing either.

Of course, there are other benefits to having the crew in new trucks too, even though pride was the main thing that motivated me at first. Another obvious upside is that a brand new, nicely painted truck acts like a billboard on wheels. Our trucks, especially, are fantastic. They are meticulously organized and wrapped in a perfect way from top to bottom.

When you're a customer and you see an A1 truck roll up to your driveway, it's impressive. It's got our mission, vision, and core values stenciled inside the door. The gear is polished and put away precisely in its place. You take one look at that truck and driver, and you know this tech is a stone-cold expert in everything relating to garage doors.

These days I tell every new employee right from orientation that our goal is to break a billion dollars per year. They know this from the beginning and wouldn't sign on to work with us if they didn't support our mission and want to help wherever possible. One of my co-workers here recently joked that it's like we've turned work into a game, and to beat the final level we must make a billion dollars in a single year. And that's a great way to think about it.

Those are some of my best ideas on competitiveness, which is the core of our culture here at A1. But there are two other major attributes to the A1 culture as well: collaboration and fun. Let's look at those too.

Second, We are Collaborative

Competition without collaboration is selfish, and that's not what we want to promote at A1. We are all about the kind of winning that lift everyone up. It's like the feeling on a sports team after you win a big tournament because everyone works together perfectly. At A1, I encourage people to be competitive and collaborative at the same time.

I am a big proponent of Simon Sinek's advice in his book, *The Infinite Game*. There is no question business owners should build a company that's going to last forever. While competition is inevitable, for me, there is no finish line. I am always setting new goals, rising to new challenges and setting new budgets.

One simple way I work toward a more collaborative feeling within the company is through language. I refer to everyone who works for A1 as my co-workers, not my employees. This language is less hierarchical and more collaborative. And I've noticed people respond well to it. A few times already in the book I've called them employees, because I wanted you to know what I was talking about. And it felt weird because I'm so used to co-workers. So, for the rest of the book I'll use the two interchangeably.

Sometimes you can promote your corporate culture through things that are insanely low tech. As a cheesy example, I recently bought aprons for some of my staff, in our company colors with A1 Garage Door Service stitched onto the front. It was funny because the home service industry is macho. So, I was walking around to these tough guys passing out aprons and we all had fun with it. There's nothing better than cooking for employees and for customers. Food brings people together in a way few things can.

Speaking of food, there's another thing I'm doing for a more collaborative culture, which also involves feeding people. I recently bought five commercial waffle irons (and they're badass). We found five-gallon buckets of waffle mix and now our breakfast setup is not to be messed with. We could legitimately feed an army. And I've been having fun with that. We make breakfast two days a week for everyone who comes in. It's been nice to connect with people.

As things heated up with the waffle irons, and we were looking for ways to get involved with the community, we hosted a "Shop With a Cop Day," and an event to honor firefighters. We have them all over for breakfast at 5am (when nothing is on fire yet). If any police officers or firefighters can't come for any reason, we deliver them waffles! Have fun with it, and find ways to get involved with the community. It turns into free marketing and great exposure for your brand. And you never know, maybe one day you'll get pulled over and the officer will remember all those delicious 5am breakfasts...just joking!

An added benefit of these types of activities designed around giving back to the community is that sometimes they can be newsworthy. Maybe local radio and TV stations hear about you feeding police officers waffles, and do stories about you. This creates a double whammy of both new customers and employees who reach out because they heard about your company on the news and thought it seemed like a positive place to do business with and work.

As a side note, when you start doing interviews for these things it's easy to get sucked into a black hole of talking about yourself and your company. Reporters ask questions like, "What inspired this?" and "How does it feel to feed cops?" and "Are you planning any other things like this?" But instead of answering in terms of yourself and your company, keep your focus on recognizing others. It plays better that way.

"Do you know what police do for us?" you might say, for example. "I am so thankful to have the Phoenix P.D. in my life, and I can't emphasize enough how deeply I appreciate everything they do to protect my friends, family, and everyone else. My co-workers and I all love giving back to these brave souls for their support of this community, so we're happy to come out at 5 am and make waffles. And if you're a business owner and you appreciate the amazing work the police do for us, you should be giving back too."

A comment like that is better than if I would have launched into talking about myself, A1, and what we do. I didn't say, "We have the best technicians," or "Our garage doors are the best in the industry," or even, "At A1 we like to make waffles for the police." Instead, I kept it all focused on the officers and I issued a challenge to other businesses to support cops too.

For me, personally, the language people use has a big impact on whether the culture feels collaborative or closed off. One thing I learned about myself is that employees should never tell me "no" they can't do something. Instead, they should say, "yes, but here's what I'm going to need…" This way I can better understand what it would take to execute the request, and I can decide whether it's worth it or not.

I hate the word "no" because, let's be honest, if you had a team of twenty people and a budget of $3 million you could find a way to fix the problem. So, "we can't do that" is a lie. It's a matter of needing more resources, not being impossible. Instead of saying "no," I would rather have people find out what it would take if we wanted to execute the plans. Maybe it's something unreasonable, in which case you can rule out that course of action. However, maybe it's possible.

Another major element of a collaborative work culture involves helping people when they're struggling. When your co-workers fail, and things don't go their way automatically, do you help each other out? Is it an environment of every-man-for-himself or we're-all-in-this-together? Can you trust that, when you're wrestling with a difficult challenge, someone will take notice and lend you a hand?

I remember when I was learning to ride a bike on our cul-de-sac in Michigan. My parents were patient, bless them. They had an interesting system to get me off training wheels. My dad grabbed both the handlebars and the back of the seat. He took off running while I pedaled frantically. Meanwhile my mom ran twenty feet up ahead. The idea was that my dad would let go and stop running, and my mom would catch me.

"Keep the handlebars straight," my dad called out as he pushed me off. But I promptly veered to the left and straight into a garbage can.

"Don't stop pedaling," my mom screamed as I tried again. This time I made it farther before crashing.

Each time I fell, they encouraged me to get back up. They never let me quit. And I knew that with the two of them running with me, dad behind me and mom in front, I was protected from serious harm. I was free to try, fall, and get back up.

Today, I'm proud to say that I can ride a bike with no training wheels.

In business, too, it's important how we respond when someone fails. It's usually best to be supportive and non-judgmental. Don't bully or belittle anyone. Support people, console them, and encourage them to get back on the bike and try again. If they don't keep trying, they will never get it. In a collaborative culture, failure is encouraged and celebrated.

Something I've found that works wonders for our company culture is for me to recognize birthdays and anniversaries for our employees. This is something I would recommend to any entrepreneur. Once per week my assistant prepares a big document with birthdays, anniversaries, and a few personalized notes about each individual. I go through and record videos for every person. Then the messages are automatically sent out on the proper days. It takes me about ten minutes and makes employees feel valued, seen, and appreciated. Try it.

In the marketing world I sometimes hear people talk about making the customer the hero of the narrative. When it comes to company culture, on the other hand, make the employee the hero. Employees are our internal customers. Without them our business would be impossible, so they are the heroes of our companies.

Make sure the collaborative aspect of your culture runs in all directions. As a company, support your employees in their life goals outside of the business, as they support the goals of the company. I led a workshop last month with our people and we brought in some amazing speakers to lead sessions. And part of the morning was that everyone had to come up with a hundred dreams they have for their lives. It was beautiful to talk with people about how we can collaborate on making their personal and professional goals come true.

Third, We have Fun

The final aspect of our culture that I've worked hard to instill is fun. I want people to enjoy working at A1 and to look forward to coming into the office each morning. Other garage door companies might be boring and serious, but not mine. Every day here is a blast, and our employees love to crack jokes, pull pranks, and lighten the mood.

It doesn't take significant planning to create a fun culture. Be willing to relax and go with the moment. If you are open to it, great opportunities for fun constantly float by, begging you to notice them. When you relax, stay present, and adopt a playful attitude, you can seize the moments and capitalize on them.

One such opportunity came along last week when I was doing some training sessions with a group of new recruits. It was a trick I learned from my good friend, Howard Partridge, who did it at a small event I attended. During one of my talks this guy went to the bathroom. And he seemed like he had a good sense of humor, so I wanted to have fun with him.

"Hey, people," I said quietly to everyone else while this guy was away, "from now on I want you all to crack up and howl with laughter any time I say 'shazam,' okay? Pretend like something absolutely hilarious happened. But don't let on to that guy in the bathroom that anything strange is going on." They all agreed.

During the rest of the day, I must have said "shazam" at least ten times. Whenever I did, everybody went crazy. And the look on this guy's face was priceless. There was obviously some joke he wasn't in on, and he was so confused about why everyone was laughing so hard. Eventually he doubled over right along with everyone else. At the end of the day, we told him what happened, and he had a big laugh about the situation.

I'd forgotten this incident, but then the other day on a training call the word "shazam" popped into my head.

"It's the exact same process we've always followed," I said. "It goes: one, two, three, 'shazam!'" Everyone died laughing. We had a blast with it.

For some reason, when people pretend to laugh, it doesn't take long for the situation to turn into honest hilarity. It's almost guaranteed to lead to fun. Try it sometime and check for yourself. One simple word, phrase, or visual cue, repeated a few times, can lighten up a dull meeting or activity. Instruct people to crack up every time they hear or see it.

During training is an especially powerful time to be deliberate about introducing activities that reflect your company culture. So, while saying "shazam" a few times might not seem like a big deal, it's important. These people saw the CEO joke around on the job and have fun during their first week here. And that's combined with everything we do to show

how competitive and collaborative we are. The result—they understand our culture right away.

One big thing I've done to make the culture more fun at A1 is change the atmosphere of the offices. My buddy Kegan came through at one point and looked around our facilities. At the time, I'm embarrassed to say I thought the place was fantastic because we had equipment and everything was state of the art. But he wasn't impressed.

"Hey man, you need a coffee maker," Kegan said in the break room, shrugging like it was the most obvious thing in the world. "And you need a soda machine." He gestured to the empty air next to the refrigerator, holding his hand out to fill an imaginary cup, and extending his finger to press an invisible button. "Also," Kegan continued, pointing toward the blank white walls, "You might start thinking about some colorful posters and artwork, to make it a better vibe for the people who come in to work here."

I glanced from the empty space on the counter, to the empty space next to the fridge, to the empty space on the walls. Wow, Kegan was right. If we were serious about making this a fun place to work, our main office couldn't be lame. We needed to fill it up with fun.

Today, I'm proud to say Kegan wouldn't recognize the place anymore. Now the office is a better reflection of the culture I want us to have. You walk through and it's obvious to see this is a fun place to work. When potential employees tour the company their jaws hit the floor at the pinball machines, Cruising USA games, and chests full of snacks. They can't help but smile when they see me there in an apron cooking everybody breakfast and lunch. That's their first introduction to our culture, before they even get hired. And that lays the groundwork for them to assimilate into the company later.

One final note on culture is that it starts with the people you hire. They have to fit the culture you're building. Not everyone is right for your company, no matter how great you are, or how awesome they are. It's better to find out earlier that someone is not a good fit. Some people come to tour our company, play pinball, eat lunch, operate machinery, see the camaraderie here, and still decide it's not right for them. That's not sad, it's what we want. Those people are not the right fit for our culture, so they are selecting themselves out of running for a job.

We have a separate recruiting process for people who are slated for positions on our executive team, and Dan Miller generally leads up those efforts. Something great Dan does when he's hiring is he makes sure to tell people all about what it's like to work with me. He paints a vivid picture of the culture surrounding me and the executive team at A1, so they can get a clear idea of whether it would be a good fit.

"Tommy is all over the place," I've overheard Dan tell a potential new executive on more than one occasion. "He's an entrepreneur. He's got ideas. If you can focus his ideas, he will be explosive. He will be a force of nature if you put him in the right spot. Take care of his advantages and help him deal with and minimize his weaknesses."

Dan realizes some people love this environment, and others hate it, but that is who I am. We hire executives who will thrive in this culture. He believes the people must fit the situation more than anything else. That's why he tells candidates all about the culture around me, trying to be as honest as possible.

"If you want to move up, work hard, and be at one of the fastest-growing companies out there," Dan tells people, "you'll never feel more passion, see more sincerity, or find someone who cares more. Also, understand Tommy is an entrepreneur, not a corporate guy. He's not going to have formal meetings. Nobody takes minutes during his meetings. That's not the way his life works. Tommy is easy to get along with. He doesn't bother you, as long as you do your job. But he might call you late at night with crazy ideas."

By describing me so specifically, Dan prepares future executives for the culture around me. They can't say they weren't warned, or that I'm more eccentric than they imagined. That's impossible because Dan makes me sound like a certifiable maniac.

"He's not a proper guy," I heard him telling a particularly important candidate the other day, standing outside my office. "If you go out to lunch, he'll order a beer."

Sometimes Dan's descriptions of me are borderline insulting. But I appreciate what he's doing. And you can't argue with the amazing string of talented C-level people he's found for us over the years. His results have been remarkable.

Tommy's Best Tips

It pays to make sure employees have a fantastic experience on their first day at work, Tommy says, so they integrate into the culture. They may have said yes to working for your company, but that doesn't mean they are fully committed to staying. They didn't take their resume down from the job boards yet. They still get messages from recruiters. The culture they experience on their first day at your company is important. It's the foundation for your relationship with them. If it doesn't go well, that's a foundation built in quicksand rather than cement.

We have it backward when it comes to hiring and retiring. Why is it that when someone resigns or retires, we have a farewell luncheon or drinks to remember their career? How come we celebrate people when they are leaving and not when they are getting started? Instead of celebrating people on the way out, we should be celebrating them on the way in, and Elevating them.

When we make a big deal about someone leaving, it sends the wrong message. We don't want to celebrate retiring. That makes other people wonder whether they should leave too. Instead, we should celebrate coming and staying.

Your culture is the one big thing that sets you apart from your competitors who also provide the same product or service. So, what's unique about it? If your people can't articulate that, it represents a lack of cohesive culture.

One of the most powerful ways to promote your culture is to get new employees to buy into it before you even hire them. Add obstacles to the application process to weed out people who lack perseverance. Make them work to show they want the job before you give it to them. This will naturally keep out the people who are less serious.

When you're in the interviewer seat, trying to find people who will be a good match for your company culture, look at the questions they ask. It can tell you a lot about where their minds are, and what kind of employees they would be.

It is a good practice in the final interview to ask, "What questions do you have for me?" Then, as a follow up, "What specifically, intrigues you about this opportunity?" It will tell a lot by how candidates respond to this. You will also learn just by the nature of their questions what their priorities are.

If they ask you about pay and future raises, you might assume they are not there for the long term. On the other hand, if they ask "What does success look like for someone in this position?" you know they are interested in their own success and a longer term relationship.

Chapter 4
The Third Pillar: Marketing

YESTERDAY I MET WITH THE OWNERS of another garage door company that has strong leadership and a great internal culture, but is struggling to hire enough quality technicians. Clearly something is missing from their formula. They want my team to look at what they are doing wrong, and figure out how to get more qualified new recruits coming in. The company is profitable and does steady eight-figure revenue.

The root of this company's issues became apparent when the CEO spoke enthusiastically about his firm dedication to keeping his marketing budget below two percent of revenue. They have some amazing direct marketing going, sending targeted mailings to hundreds of thousands of homes. And it's a cheap way to find customers. But, in their quest to slash pennies from the marketing budget, the company failed to consider the hidden back side of marketing—the side that gets your brand's image and reputation in front of prospective employees and business partners. When marketing is focused only on customers, and not the back side, you struggle.

"You've been here in Phoenix for a few days," I said excitedly, looking for a good way to explain the concept to them. "Have you seen some of our marketing? It's practically everywhere."

"Oh, right," said the CEO awkwardly, "those." I noticed chuckles and eye rolls from a few people on his team.

"What have you seen?" I asked, looking for more information.

"The billboards," one of his people said. "Well, it's...they just say 'A1 Garage Door' and have a picture of Tommy's face."

"Right," said someone else, "they don't even have a phone number!

Nobody is ever going to see the billboard, look up your number, and call from their car. It doesn't make sense."

"Ahh, I see what you mean," I said. "I see how that could be confusing. Let me explain. See, the customers don't call from their car on the freeway. They call from the garage when it's broken. That's when they remember all those billboards they've been seeing for years. And they look up 'A1 Garage Door,' and give us a call.

"But, what's even more important to understand," I continued, "is that those billboards aren't only for customers. Those are for everybody. This is the back side of marketing. See, your direct response mailings are efficient for finding customers. But they don't find you employees, partners, or investors. They have no back side."

To illustrate this idea, I pointed to Larry, the newest A1 team member in the room.

"Here's a phenomenal new guy we hired a couple months ago," I said. "Larry, what attracted you to apply?"

"I saw Tommy and A1 everywhere," he shrugged. "I figured there must be something amazing going on there that I needed to be a part of."

As the people from this other company watched Larry talk, I could see recognition dawning on their faces. I was glad to help them learn a lesson that cost me years of expensive trial and error to understand myself. Marketing is not only about finding employees. It's critical for attracting A-players to come work with you.

The company was struggling because they were so focused on keeping their marketing spending under two percent. Their mindset was that they couldn't possibly spend a cent more on marketing because they couldn't raise their prices any higher, or because they were already charging the standard market rate. The only solution they could see was to cut expenditures as low as possible. They believed they could only turn a profit by keeping every spending category within a narrow band. This led them to overlook the back side of marketing.

When most people think about marketing, we ignore half of the picture. We focus on the front side, or how marketing attracts new customers to our brand. But we overlook the back side, or how it also brings us new employees and partners. If you do this right, you should have two lines of people outside of your door, one waiting to buy from you and the other applying to work with you.

Of course, you want to attract the right people to apply for jobs with you, not the wrong ones. So clearly define the type of person you're looking for. When you get clear on what you stand for as a company, you can create marketing that attracts employees who share your values.

Before he became one of the world's leading experts on how to build a cutting-edge marketing magnet to attract a stream of phenomenal employees into a company, Jody Underhill was an executive at a power company in Florida. Over the course of twenty-six years, he worked his way up to the role of Director of Executive and National Account who reported directly to the Vice President of Customer Service for a big Fortune 250 company. On the surface, he was successful and had a great life. But deep down he felt burnt out and bored. He realized he was going through the motions.

Eventually, Jody decided he'd had enough with his corporate career, and he left to start a marketing agency. This would be the adventure he'd always dreamed of. He'd be the captain of his own ship, traveling the world to attend conferences and speak at events.

At one of those events, he met me, Tommy Mello. I came up to him and introduced myself after his talk on marketing. We connected that day and have been friends ever since.

A few years into running his agency, Jody was back to having many of the same problems he'd been facing in the corporate world. He was getting burned out. He was putting in long days, working weekends, traveling to new cities every week, going to different conferences, and speaking on stage, which was exciting but also draining. But his main income was from his local business marketing services. In addition to all his other activities, he had to deal with dozens of clients—none of them had a big budget and all of them were very demanding.

Then someone reached out to ask for help. Jody's friend Tosh, was in the trucking business, and he had a big problem. He was about to lose some huge clients because he didn't have enough competent drivers to deliver on the contracts he was signing. He was desperate to find more high-quality drivers in a matter of days and onboard them immediately.

Jody saw an opportunity both to help his friend, and also try his hand at a new aspect of marketing. It was a nice change of pace from his other projects, and he threw himself full force into the recruiting challenge. He thought carefully about how to take the principles that he knew worked to attract customers and modify them for new employees instead. He developed video ads, tested landing pages, set up automations, and bought traffic. He innovated with technologies that are standard in marketing, but not in recruiting.

The campaign worked and the men located some amazing candidates. Jody was able to save all but one of the contracts that were in danger of being lost. In less than a week he'd hired four excellent drivers who all ended up staying for years. But, more importantly, he discovered the back side of marketing, an area most business owners neglect. He'd stumbled upon the idea of using the latest ad technology to recruit superstar employees. And it worked.

Jody realized this could be a great business for him. After all, there are hundreds of thousands of trucking companies in the United States alone. He started cold outreach on LinkedIn and had twelve clients in the first month. That's when he knew this was something big, and he officially shifted his focus away from marketing every kind of local business. Instead, he focused specifically on helping trucking companies find great new employees.

A few months later I got a call from Jody.

"Hey Tommy," he said excitedly, "you gotta check out what we're doing here in trucking. You're gonna wanna see this right away."

There are few people in the world who talk faster than I do, and Jody is one of them. Talking with him is like "drinking from a firehose," as he often jokes. I struggled to follow everything he was saying, but his excitement was electrifying, and I knew he wouldn't be calling me unless this was important.

I was at the airport, on the way home from a conference, and it was tough to hear him over the ambient sounds. Elevator music hummed away in the background. Boarding announcements punctuated the soundtrack every few seconds. Screaming children played tag a few feet from my face. And I was tired.

Whatever he wanted to show me was clearly important, so I did something impulsive and switched my ticket to stop in South Carolina and see him that afternoon. A few hours later he picked me up from the airport and we were on the way to his office. Jody has this way of looking at you that feels like he's always winking, even though he's not. It's a playful exuberance that spills out of him and flows in every direction.

What Jody showed me at his office that day was miles beyond any recruiting system I'd ever seen. He was using high-level marketing tactics like follow-up sequences, SMS text reminders, and social media ads. Everything was so dialed-in and on-target, I couldn't believe it.

"I want this for my business," I said.

"I knew you would," he nodded. "But it's highly experimental. I've only done it for a few trucking companies. We've never applied it to any other industry."

Within two weeks the system was up at A1, and we had ads running. The results were immediate and astounding. Before then, our HR team struggled to find five new techs per week. With Jody's system in place, that jumped to over twenty qualified new technicians per week right away.

Over the following months we continued to tweak and refine the system. We tested each aspect in many different ways to determine what worked best. We developed templates and samples for every step of the process. Now it's been a year and the system is dialed-in to an insane level.

As word got out about what he did for us at A1, and for those trucking companies, Jody got calls from people in other industries too, asking for the same kind of system. He started a company called RapidHirePro that specializes in implementing the process, to help businesses of all sizes automate their recruiting efforts. Right now, he's focused on industries where companies hire technicians, since it's one of the most difficult roles to recruit for today. But in the future, he plans to apply this approach to many other businesses, too. It works for nearly everything.

Now Jody focuses on the hidden back side of marketing. He's realized good advertisements are not only about acquiring new customers, but also about getting the right people to work for you. If you do that, it's crazy what can happen. My top guy does $3 million per year, and most people in the garage door industry would say it's impossible to do more than $1 million. But I have a guy who does three. That's the magic of matching the right person to the perfect role.

Often in business we ignore the hidden back side of marketing. And then we wonder why we don't have amazing employees lining up outside our doors. The solution is to get scientific with how you go about advertising your company as a great place to work.

Manage Your Own Media

In today's marketplace most people will form a first impression of your brand online well before they come across your product or service in the real world. Modern consumers are exceptionally good at sizing up a company from a quick scan through social media. If we want to influence their first impression of us, we must join the conversation and get proactive on these platforms.

But it's not only social media that will influence someone's first impression of your company. In today's world, everyone will Google you before they come in for an interview. What are they going to find? Be in control of what people see when they look you up online. If things are coming up that you don't manage, that could be a problem.

Here at A1 Garage Door, almost everyone who comes in for an interview mentions that they watched about twenty-five videos on our social media. They say things like "You clearly have such a great culture" or "I love what you guys are doing here."

Our online presence has been shaping their perceptions of our brand already, long before they ever set foot in our headquarters for their interview. By the time they arrive, they are excited. I don't want people to walk on eggshells, but I want them to feel like when they step through these doors, this is Top Gun. This is where the best hang out.

Market your company as an awesome place to work. Depict your typical employee as an aspirational archetype. Post videos showing co-workers having fun together. Your ideal applicant will see these clips and feel like people at your company are cool and fun to hang out with.

Clearly define your values if you want to attract the right people. You can't skip this step. What do you want people to say about you?

Imagine a grassy hilltop with low gray clouds and light rain. Everything feels muffled and wet, like the world is far away. People in dark clothing gather soberly, and there is a coffin at the front of the crowd. Sitting inside is your corpse. And all around are photos from your life. Everyone who loved you is here.

As the afternoon unfolds and people make comments, what do you hope they will say about you and your company? What do you wish people would admire about you and be grateful for? Spend time visualizing this hilltop scene and writing down everything you hope people will say.

Now return to the present moment and think about how to market your company today, to attract the type of people who can make it into the kind of place that will be remembered the way you want years down the road. What kind of a team will it take to achieve the things you saw people saying up on the hill? And what type of organization, with what type of values, would attract people like that?

At my own funeral, I want the message to be that I helped other people win. I want to inspire and empower others to be Number 1 in their personal and professional lives. I will hire employees at my companies who also value winning and enjoy helping others win. We are competitive but also giving, not selfish. This came from thinking deeply through the funeral exercise.

One thing about this way of marketing is that, when you get good at it, you can market to new employees and customers at the same time. For instance, you could do a radio ad that says something like "Are you sick of your everyday life? Are you ready for a change? We're looking for the best, most motivated, community-driven people to join our team. If you value learning, growth, and giving back to help others win, you're our kind of employee. Join A1 Garage Door today!" Potential employees might hear the ad and apply. Also, potential customers might be listening and thinking, "Wow, sounds like a nice company." Next month when their garage door breaks, who will they call?

Be careful you don't accidentally appeal to the wrong values with the messaging you put into the world. Use the right bait to attract your ideal employee. Don't say the wrong thing.

If my business was called "Discount Garage Door, Lowest Price Guaranteed!" I would attract a different kind of customer and employee than I do being called A1 and charging a premium rate. Ask yourself where an A-player would want to work. What would they look for in a job? Figure that out and position yourself in that way when you write up your ad.

Where to post your ad online is different depending on your typical customers and employees. My avatar spends time hanging out on Instagram, TikTok, YouTube, and Snapchat. Being in those places gives me the best chance of getting exposed to as many people as possible who might be a good fit. My customers, on the other hand, are fifty- and sixty-something-year-old homeowners. They hang out in different places online, like Facebook, Nextdoor, Instagram, and Google.

In addition to being in the right places, it also helps to know what your target employee archetype is looking for and present yourself in that way. Adjust how you refer to the company so your ad will appeal to the people you want to attract for jobs. This is especially true in the world of online marketing because hiring law stipulates that you can't discriminate against who you show your ad to. So, everyone will see it. But the people who click are the ones you're looking for. You also want those people tagging their friends and partners if they see it as an opportunity for them.

I was talking to our head HR person the other day and we were discussing our hiring strategy.

"What would happen if I took a marshmallow," I said, "put it on a hook at the end of a pole, and dropped it in the water?"

"Nothing," she shot me a confused look. "Fish don't eat marshmallows."

"OK," I responded. "Well, what if I put a nice juicy worm on there with a weight, and dropped it down two feet?"

"Yeah," she nodded, breaking into a smile and rolling her eyes, "then you might catch a fish, Tommy. That's what you'd typically use for bait and tackle around here."

"Perfect," I said. "So, isn't higher than average pay better bait and tackle to attract A-players to our company than average pay while they're in training? Is average pay the right bait for a company that wants to attract some of the best and most ambitious people in America?"

"You're right," she shrugged. "It's like average pay is a marshmallow if you're trying to catch a real winner."

Shazam!

Never Stop Searching

One place many companies go wrong, in my opinion, is in viewing recruiting as a Human Resources task. Let the HR department focus on making life great for people inside the company. Recruiting should be its own separate department with a director of recruiting who understands that marketing goes hand in hand with recruiting. Because just like marketing, you should always be recruiting.

Seriously, there is no time, that if the right person walked along, you shouldn't get that individual on the bus right away.

Why do we view marketing as something we should do all the time to drive brand awareness, but we don't think the same about recruiting? The way most business owners treat recruiting is more like a discrete task than an ongoing process. If there are job openings, we recruit. As soon as we fill them up, we stop. Whew, nice to be done with that for a while. Except, that's the wrong attitude. Recruiting is a vital function, and we should keep it going all the time.

I'm always recruiting, and you should be, too. In the checkout line at the grocery store, I'm recruiting. At the hot new restaurant in town, I'm recruiting. Heck, I'm even recruiting when the roofer comes by to fix my shingles. Any time I come across someone motivated and handy, I ask about what they do for work. If they express interest in a new career, I'm right there with a business card. Similarly, when people ask what I do, that's a chance to describe A1 as an amazing family and try to entice people to ask for my business card. I don't want to force it on them. I want them to ask.

If I meet an awesome busboy, I go to work recruiting him to join my company. Every day when he goes in there to bus those tables I want him to think, I wonder if I'd be better off going with that Tommy guy. I don't know anything about garage doors, but maybe I should go out and meet with him and do a ride along, like he said. I've found if I approach people a few times and keep the lines open, they will usually reach out at some point and tell me they want to come over to A1. People might be happy right now, but they won't always be. If you stay in touch, they will reach out when they get sick of their old job and are ready for a change.

It's also good, when you talk with people, to be obvious you're recruiting them to work for you. Be pushy about this, it's not annoying. It's flattering. People will come over to your company if you show how interested you are in them. We all want to work for someone who appreciates us.

Many business owners will hand people a card and say, "Call me if you're ever looking for a job." That's typical. But you can be more aggressive and say something like, "Hey, come do a ride-along with me next Thursday so I can show you how working for A1 will change your life for the better." If someone is interested, I close them on the next step while I have the chance. And the next step in our industry is a ride-along. I sign people up for one of those on the spot.

Then I follow up the next week, then the following week, then the third week with a question mark. I think it's important to be persistent. I think when you keep following up, people are like "Wow, this guy's really serious." Maybe they'll have a bad day at work and say, "I'm actually going to do this."

Salespeople sometimes talk about how important it is to believe in the product you're selling. It's hard to sell something you think is a waste of money. The same is true for recruiting. You aren't motivated to recruit new people into the company if you're worried it's going to be a circus once they sign up and get going. Why would employees convince their friends to join if management doesn't have their own heads on straight?

Good marketing, therefore, begins with treating your current people right. When you make sure the company is an awesome place to work, your employees will be sure to tell their friends. It's also important they get recognition of some kind for those referrals, whether it's money or prizes or a trip, for bringing in someone new. That's why the Leadership and Culture pillars come before Marketing. If it's not great to work for you, nobody is going to go out of their way to recommend the job to a friend. Nobody wants to recruit their friends into something sketchy.

This goes both ways, too. You don't want to settle for hiring the first people you meet who seem like they can handle the work. If you hire people because they say they can do a job, they'll work for your money. But if you hire people who believe what you believe, they'll work for you with blood, sweat, and tears.

Recruiting is about more than finding people with certain skills. It's about building a tribe. You can teach anyone whatever skills you need them to know. But do they share the values of the tribe? Would their personality be a good addition to the energy of the team?

One guy told me he was doing all this advertising on social media. Then he would only get ten applications, and seven wouldn't show up for the interview. The three that did show up were terrible. But he had to hire somebody. This business owner was blaming the candidates for being terrible. But maybe he wasn't clear on his values, or why his company is an amazing place to work. Or maybe his pay was not competitive, or his ads looked too generic. Attracting the right talent is the responsibility of the person hiring—not the person looking to be hired.

Winners Referring Winners

They say like attracts like. I've read that people are most similar to their five closest friends. So, if we have a team of winners, and we're looking for more A-players like them, where should we start our search? Why not look for even more ways to tap into our employees' social and familial networks? Winners hang out with other winners. It's a simple formula.

My philosophy is to turn the whole company into the recruiting department. We offer incentives for finding new employees, and we teach our people how to post about us on social media, refer to us in conversations, and get credit for their referrals. We have over six hundred co-workers, and I realized that if they could all give out one business card per week, or make one social media post, that would solve the recruiting question.

I asked myself how I could turn every employee into a recruiter. And I saw a few challenges to making it work. First, I had to teach every single employee how to recruit people into the company. And this might be different for every role. I needed a Learning Management System and training videos. Second, I had to develop KPIs and systems for tracking performance and rewarding people who made referrals.

With any big new project, it's nice to start with easy wins (because often things turn out harder than you expect). Instead of launching a company-wide program, you can start with a pilot using a small group of co-workers who are most excited about it. One simple strategy for prioritizing people to focus on helping to build your employee referral program is to look for who has a big reach. There will be people who are into social media, blogging, and podcasting. Develop systems and guides to teach them how to recruit for you. This will yield the biggest immediate results, since these employees already have built-in audiences. When you can get your workforce to promote the company on social media, that's when things get magical.

You'll also have people who prefer to recruit through face-to-face interactions, rather than social media. Don't count employees out as recruiters merely because they don't have a huge TikTok presence. I like to put people into a group to learn pitching skills and set up to recruit through any organizations they belong to. Everyone has at least one group outside of the office where they can promote the company. Maybe they are involved with a church choir or little league, or their wife is a realtor, or their daughter is the school valedictorian, or their son is the number one football player. We all have lives outside of work, and we are all members of various communities. These are all pools where people could be drawing from to find your new employees. They aren't as obvious or as instant as social media followings, but they can be extremely valuable if you get employees to pitch your opportunity to the group.

It's a good idea to specifically help employees identify opportunities to network and teach them how to promote the company in different situations and to different types of people. If you sit down with your co-workers and find out where they hang out, what they do on social media, what they watch, and what they read, you could find a way to make them all promoters for your company.

Don't be afraid to get as specific as hosting workshops and walking your people step-by-step through what you want them to post. I provide my co-workers with templates and sample posts they can easily use with zero effort. My goal is to equip people to win. I want to Elevate them.

It's also a good idea to combine instruction with incentives for the most valuable behaviors. In my case, I offer everyone in the company $1,500 for each new person they refer who joins our team. Then I put together explainer videos on the best, most proven strategies to recruit a few friends to join A1. This way we pair instruction and incentives together.

Even with these guides for every department, don't underestimate the power of random reminders. Everyone at my company knows they're going to get $1,500 if they refer someone who comes to work with us. It's common knowledge here. But still, sometimes on the weekends I send around reminders, with instructions for how to blast an announcement out via social media. That always brings in some applications.

I've realized my employees won't get good results posting about the company online if I don't show them how to post and what to say. I can't expect them to be social media wizards. My job is to equip everybody to win. This is an easy way they can score $1,500 if I give them tools to succeed. If I have employees who want to recruit some friends and earn the bonus, but aren't able to do it, then I failed. I didn't give them enough resources to win.

One employee recruited ten new hires during the final quarter of last year. Since we promised people $1,500 per referral, we owed him money. I decided to make a big deal out of it. I gave him one of those giant checks and filmed the whole thing. Then I posted the videos all over social media so everyone on my team could see how much money they missed out on by not posting about our job openings as aggressively as this guy.

When you give people the tools to succeed you can have a more direct conversation with them. You can say, "Hey, look at this guy who paid attention to those emails where I told you what to post on social media to recruit your friends. He made $15,000. You could be earning a commission, too, if you followed the instructions I'm sending out."

Many thousands of people have watched the video I posted on Facebook of me personally awarding this guy his huge check. Hopefully that will motivate them to pay more attention next time I send around a random reminder with some templates and examples for what they can post.

If you ask big companies where their best employees come from, they will all say referrals. When great people bring their friends to come work for you, the result is usually more great people. If your employees have their recruiter hats on at all times as they go about their days, you can count on great applicants.

The most important thing about a referral program is that it has to be fair. If people aren't confident they will get paid, why would they refer anyone? Imagine if you went to all the trouble to promote the company and convince a friend to apply, and then you didn't get your bonus when the person signed up. Would you ever refer another person again? That one bonus might not seem like a big deal, but it could be the difference between an employee who goes on and refers tons of people, or stops at one.

Posts from friends on social media are a great way to learn about job opportunities, so don't discount this. We are all bombarded by so many random opportunities every day that it's hard to tell what's legitimate. So, when we see something recommended by someone we know, that gets our attention.

Put some resources behind creating assets for your company and helping employees and other stakeholders to share and promote them. You can recommend ten different Facebook and Instagram posts. Teach them what to send in an email or text and what to post on LinkedIn. Many business owners miss a huge opportunity by not telling employees how to post about the company on social media. If you make cool content and your people all know how to reshare it, you can amplify the reach of a small advertising budget.

Advertise Yourselves

Reviews are another form of social proof that doesn't feel like marketing because they are written organically by customers or employees. These are now a huge part of how people shop for anything online, including jobs. Many hungry people turn to reviews on Google and Yelp when deciding where to get dinner. When it comes to finding the right job, seekers look for reviews on Glassdoor and Indeed. If your company has been in business for a while, employees will leave reviews on these sites about their experiences working for you. So, check what's out there and make sure it's amazing. If it's not, make it right.

Many entrepreneurs don't regularly check product reviews to see what customers are saying, and that's a missed opportunity. However, even more business owners have never gone to see what employees say about their experiences with the organization. Are you checking your reviews? Do you know what employees say about working for you? Don't conduct a survey to find out. The information is freely available online.

To attract people to your company, tell the right story. Stories sell. One author who got me thinking about how to do this is Donald Miller in his book *Building a StoryBrand*. I make a habit of sharing success stories and gathering testimonial from my employees. If they've had amazing experiences with me, I want everyone to know. I'm proud to say some of our people have completely turned their lives around and they are proud to share that with other. This is particularly useful when you are trying to attract new employees. They want to work for a company with people who are happy and are thriving.

Strangely, most recruiting ads I see in the industry look more like a prison sentence than an exciting opportunity. "Must show up on time," they demand. "Background check required," they proclaim. "Highly punctual candidates only," they rudely declare. Wow, so many barriers. And not one mention of what makes this an incredible opportunity for the applicant. Isn't the reader fantastically lucky to be looking for a job right now, when this amazing role happens to be open? Aren't there fabulous perks and a sensational team culture? Sell it.

We did some marketing at Top Golf that was successful. It's a bar and golf driving range that keeps score, similar to a bowling alley. Competitive and athletic people hang out there, so I thought it might be our crowd. We made up some posters and tried to put ourselves in the applicant's shoes and think of what would be appealing to them.

The posters we ended up going with are absolutely killing it. They simply say, "No experience. No four-year degree. Flexible hours. Clear path to six figures in your first year." Turns out that's what people want to know if they are going to pursue any kind of opportunity. Then they will go research you online, so whatever pops up is important.

Keep repeating the mantra that your job is to help everyone else at your company win. That's the key that makes everything else work. If you only remember one thing from this book, make it that.

"Guys," I told my team during training, "if you ever realize you're not having fun, come to me and resign. I don't want you to ever not like it here. I want you all to be homeowners. I want you to have the best credit scores. I want you to go on those dream vacations. I want you to be the best father or mother you could possibly be."

Make sure you've got a nice employee benefits presentation, especially in this day and age. As the competition for top talent heats up, benefits are becoming increasingly important. Companies are looking for ways to distinguish themselves from their competitors as awesome places to work. A polished benefits presentation can give you that extra edge.

While it used to be appropriate to use the word "hiring," it now makes more sense to refer to the same activity as "recruiting." Managers used to think, "I'm the boss. They have to come in and apply to work for me." But it doesn't work that way anymore. Today, great employees don't come to you.

Stay on the lookout for opportunities to get into the community and make connections. It's worth paying for these kinds of things, in my experience. For instance, I had two requests on my desk this week to sponsor local sports teams. It's about $1,000 and they feature your logo in their programs.

I told them I'll do it if they agree to post a video on their website of me saying, "Hi, I'm Tommy Mello, founder of A1 Garage Door Service, and we gave to support the football team because we care, and you should give too." This way I can promote A1 but mostly keep it focused on the organization and encouraging others to give. It should have a link back to our website—however they post it.

On the topic of school outreach, here's a letter I recently sent out to high school sports coaches in my area. It included a gift card inside for free coffee.

Dear Coach,

I wanted to take a minute to introduce myself. My name is Tommy Mello, owner of A1 Garage Door Service.

Firstly, I cannot tell you how much I respect the fact that you are coaching at Andover High School. Thank you for making the world a better place and showing the youth what life is all about. It's admirable to say the least, great job.

Recently I had an epiphany about recruiting: good high school coaches could direct us to students they know who might be interested in a great paying career with paid time off, room for advancement, and an amazing culture.

We're looking for candidates who want to win, exceed customer expectations, be team players, and just plain have fun.

In my youth I was involved in gymnastics, karate, swimming, baseball, soccer, wrestling, football, and so many more sports. I realize you probably know several perfect candidates who fit the A1 winning attitude.

About A1 Garage Door Service. We won the Inc growth award for our industry four years in a row. We hire up from within. We plan on making the experience more than a job, rather, a career. We are huge on promotion of our culture, meaning we enjoy barbecues, bowling trips, Top Golf, and many other things to help grow the team. Our vision is to become North America's largest and most trusted garage door company. Right now, we have over 600 employees.

The process is simple. First, the candidate would go for a ride-along to see if it's a perfect fit. Then we'll fast-track them through our apprentice program and fly them out to our national training center in Phoenix. There they learn as much as possible and return as a Junior Tech. They have the opportunity to rise in rank every quarter, to Tech, then Senior Tech, and, within a year, Field Tech, at a six-figure income level.

We would love to see if you'll spread the word for us to anybody you know. We are giving $1,000 to whichever school's team sends in the most candidates. The best *candidates for us are twenty years or older, with a good driving record and can pass a background check and driving test.*

Most importantly, have fun, work hard, and strive to be #1.

Coffee is on us today.

Best wishes,
Tommy Mello
Founder / CEO
A1 Garage Door Service

My goal is to have as many people sending me A-players as possible. So, I try to maintain relationships with anyone who might have my type of candidate coming across their desk. But the biggest place we get new candidates from is those ads Jody set up.

In fact, when COVID hit and most other businesses cut back on advertising, we tripled down, because we knew our model worked. We also knew our other pillars were working fine. Don't rev up your marketing spend until you have the other four pillars working too, it doesn't do anything on its own.

Jody Underhill's Best Tips

Now that he's becoming one of the foremost authorities in the world on how to market your business to prospective employees, Jody has a lot to say on the topic. I asked him to share tips on what he's learned by running hiring campaigns for hundreds of brands.

Keep in mind, he said, that seventy-four percent of people are passive job seekers. They don't actively build profiles on job posting websites, but they would be open to a new opportunity if it came along. When you go to the job boards, you're only getting people with resumes. But seventy percent of the people who apply through social media don't have resumes. As a result, when you post on typical recruiting sites you only get a small percentage of people on the job market at any given time.

Don't go fishing in the same place as everyone else. Avoid the common job sites.

Instead of thinking about the challenge like a recruiter, approach it like a marketer. You're selling people a new job. Like a marketer, Jody thinks in terms of images, videos, headlines, and copy. He wants to optimize these elements to generate an ad that gets the best candidates possible to apply.

In the text of your ads, Jody says, lead with the benefits of the job, rather than the requirements. The way most people advertise for employees is the equivalent of a contractor saying, "I'm looking for clients with an over 5,000 square foot house and a perfect credit score. We'll come over and do repairs." Imagine if you saw a plumber with this kind of advertising.

The way you phrase things in your ads is important. Say, "performance pay" instead of "commission only," because it sounds better. People like the idea they can make more money if they perform better, but they don't like the idea of not having a base salary. Small changes in wording make a big difference. Test a variety of ways to phrase everything.

Don't bombard people with information in your first ad. Intrigue them to click and opt in. Then you can send them more info. With social media ads, you'll catch people at random times, when they happen to be scrolling through for a few seconds. It's not realistic to ask them to stop and fill out the application right then and there. Instead, use the platform's one-click opt-in feature to quickly get their email address and cell phone number. Now you can send them a link to the application.

As soon as people apply, they should get dropped into an automation sequence where you'll give them more information about the benefits of the job, answer their questions, and remind them to complete their application. Jody sends a new message every day until a person finishes the application. First, he texts them a photo of the ad they clicked, to remind them who it is. Then he talks to them as an individual. For instance, with A1, his software texts them as me saying, "Hey, it's Tommy Mello, the founder of A1 Garage Door!"

The messages you send to applicants are often going to be some of their first real exposure to your brand. Make sure the messages reflect your company values. Show them it's a fun place to work. For example, on Day 4 Jody sends a photo of my dog, Finnegan. And it says he gets a treat for every application completed. On Day 5 it's a picture of Tom Cruise hanging from the ceiling, and it says, "Your mission, should you choose to accept it, is to fill out your application. This message will self-destruct in five seconds."

The landing page you send people to is important as well. In the hiring world this is generally referred to as the application page, but in marketing we think of it as a sales page. This is where we sell them on applying for the job. One important feature of a good sales page is there aren't any alternative options to click on. The only thing you can do is move forward in the process. An application page is the same way. It should discuss the benefits of the job and then allow them to apply. That's it. The conversion rate on this application page goes up thirty-four percent when there is some kind of video on the page. You can even film something basic using your computer's webcam.

Once they submit the application, Jody invites candidates to complete a video interview. This is a great step because it is automated. He uses software that asks candidates questions and films their responses for a pre-set amount of time. They don't get re-dos. Then someone from Jody's team watches the videos to get a feel for the candidates. This helps weed people out without a significant effort or time investment.

Something more advanced Jody has discovered recently involves how to target your ads to people with the right level of experience. Of course, you can't exclude certain people from seeing an ad. All you can do is adjust the way you phrase things. When you want someone with more experience, show how they will have a better quality of life if they switch to your company. Tell them you have newer trucks, dispatch from home, more vacation time, no on-call, a steady stream of jobs, and good work-life balance.

On the other hand, if you want someone less experienced, but with a good attitude and eagerness to learn, use a different approach. Position your marketing more like, "Are you ready for a new career?" Because that's what you're offering people with this opportunity. You're going to teach them a trade. This is a career if they want it to be, not only a job.

The biggest thing to keep in mind, Jody says, is that you can always improve your marketing. He still learns new things every day, even though he's been doing this for years. There are constantly new discoveries that surprise him.

Don't get arrogant. Stay curious. Over seventy percent of companies feel they do a good job communicating during the hiring process, but only twenty-seven percent of applicants agree. If you think you're doing well, don't be so sure. You can always improve your messaging.

Chapter 5
The Fourth Pillar: Recruiting

WHEN YOU HAVE A CONSISTENT SYSTEM FOR GETTING A-players on the bus, and for giving them the tools to win, your business will explode. Recruiting is a huge part of that. Once you've got an electric culture and people respond to your help wanted ads, what next? How do you find the best candidates and hire them? Should you poach your competitors' employees? What about when you need experienced people for management and C-level positions?

One of the biggest mistakes business owners make early on is focusing too narrowly on hiring for exact skills and experience. While this is the right approach when looking for leadership positions, it places huge limitations when hiring technicians, CSRs, or dispatchers. Also, what if you can't find enough people with the right experience? What if those people are too expensive? What if they all do things differently since they were trained at other companies with different protocols? This, it turns out, is a trap.

My friend Danny Kerr has the perfect story for us to look at and learn from. When he first started his painting business, he found himself caught in the trap of hiring for skills over attitude. It wasn't long before he reached a make-or-break moment in the growth of the company. He'd lost three new hires, leaving him with multiple customers waiting for work and no one to complete it. "It was at that moment," Danny later recalled, "that I realized, 'Man, I can't keep running things from the hip.' The way I was running things wasn't scalable." If he couldn't fix the holes in his business, he would be stuck doing the work himself. Or else he could refund the customers' deposits and cancel the jobs. He'd tried to hire the perfect people, but couldn't find anyone with the right experience.

So, he snapped up the first guys who responded to his ads on Craigslist. However, his training sessions with the team weren't going well. In fact, his last session got him into this pickle.

Danny had hired six new painters and scheduled a month's worth of work for each of them. They were all waiting for him at the facility, ready to learn his process. But Danny was running late. As he rushed in his van to the facility, his ladders loosened their holds on the roof. They hung by threads on either side of the vehicle as he pulled in, banging noisily. Embarrassed, Danny exited the van and greeted his new employees. Then he opened the side door, and three paint cans fell out, cracking open on the concrete and spilling paint everywhere. Three of his new hires left on the spot.

As bad as his problems were, Danny was going to learn something about recruiting that would revolutionize his business. His immediate impulse was to take on the jobs himself and sort everything else out later. After all, the clients were waiting. And he could do the work himself if he dropped everything else. But his mentor advised against this.

"If you don't stop and fill those holes now," Danny's mentor told him, "you'll never fill them and you'll always be working. You'll never grow. Set yourself up for long term success." Trusting his advisor, Danny called the customers, pushed their jobs back a couple weeks, and bought himself time to recruit a few high-quality painters. As Michael Gerber, a business skills trainer and author of several books, says, "Work ON the business, not IN it."

But Danny quickly ran into problems. He'd never had to hire reliable employees so quickly before. In the past, applicants trickled in organically whenever he needed new people. This was a different problem. How was he going to find, hire, and train three great new painters in only two weeks?

First, he posted ads on the typical job sites. But after a couple days no strong applicants came through. Danny was a wreck. He dreaded checking his inbox for new alerts. The mere thought of doing so caused his heart rate to spike. Nobody who applied was anywhere near experienced enough.

Out of options, Danny decided he couldn't afford to wait for the perfect employees to come along. He hired the three most motivated people he could find and got aggressive with training, coaching, and mentoring them. He developed learning materials, lectured, gave pop quizzes, demonstrated proper techniques, observed his people in the field, and more.

The three painters Danny hired and trained that week all turned out amazing. They finished every job, and he didn't lose a single one. After training those guys, Danny hired more painters, making sure they were highly motivated and putting them all through the same intense learning process.

There are many lessons to learn from Danny's story, but one of the most basic things he got right with his formula is shifting his focus from experience to motivation. It wasn't working to search for people with the skills he needed. Danny hired for attitude instead. And he took on the responsibility of teaching everyone the skills.

That was a major turning point.

Keep this as your core mantra: Hire A-players and Elevate them to win. You don't want to hire the wrong people. You're looking for winners.

As Danny discovered that day, one A-player is worth more than three B-players. When three people abandoned him in his time of trouble, he realized it's better to have one person who stays than three who disappear at the first sign of challenge.

See, he might have hired those quitters, but he didn't recruit them. There is a difference. If the applicants coming in are unemployed that's different from if they are in-demand. It's easy to find people nobody wants. The hard people to find are the ones everyone wants. That's the challenge of recruiting.

As a bonus, when you recruit someone who is killing it at their current job, they often bring a few other A-players with them during the following months. They talk about how great their new job is to their old buddies, one thing leads to another, and soon the whole team moves over to your side of the fence.

What works best, I've found, is to develop a process for recruiting and run it constantly. This way you can have a steady flow of applicants. Also, you can hone your process over time by making tweaks and monitoring your results to see whether things get better or worse.

The worst thing you can do is jump into something massive, like recruiting without a clear process. I've done that before. It occurs when we're getting into something huge, but we don't think it's a big deal. That's what happened to Colonel George Armstrong Custer at the Battle of Little Bighorn in 1876. He thought it would be no problem for his men on horseback with guns to defeat the final armies from the Sioux, Cheyenne, and Arapaho tribes. Instead of waiting for reinforcements, as he was advised, the young Colonel decided to rush in and finish the natives off while he had the obvious upper hand. That battle is known as Custer's Last Stand.

These days, I assume things are going to be more complicated than I can possibly imagine, and nowhere has that been truer than when it comes to recruiting. We have a robust hiring system at A1, and it's constantly evolving. First, there are multiple interviews. Then we send an official offer letter and conduct a background check and personality profile. Then the candidate has to do some "ride-alongs." It's an in-depth process purposefully because mistakes are expensive. But it's not overly cumbersome.

In recruiting there is the question of how wide to go in the types of experience you consider relevant. Most business owners in my industry mainly look for people who have already been salespeople or technicians in closely related fields. But I've found many great people from the hospitality industry, casino industry, and all kinds of service roles. Whether someone worked at a movie theater, a bowling alley, a bar, or a hotel, it doesn't matter as long as they are good at dealing with people.

So, don't limit yourself. Get creative and find ways to search for people who are good problem solvers. Look for employees with a competitive drive who love to win. And don't worry about finding someone with the exact experience you're looking for. Give them basic tests and then leave it up to them to decide whether they want to try out the job.

How to Spot a Winner

From the company's perspective hiring is risky. We invest a considerable amount of money into a new employee before they are hired, onboarded, trained, and fully productive. Choosing the wrong person can be an expensive and time-consuming error. The U.S. Department of Labor estimates that the average cost of a bad hiring decision costs at least thirty percent of the individual's first year of expected earnings. There are other costs, too, from a disrupted company culture, decreased work production, and possible loss of customers and revenue. How can we tell while we're recruiting someone, whether they're going to end up being an A-player or not?

One of the easy things to look for is whether someone knows how to finish things. It's obvious when you're talking to someone with a pattern of quitting projects partway through. For instance, the fact that someone dropped out of college doesn't mean anything on its own. But if you also see a huge gap in their curriculum and other indications of lack of commitment, it might look more like a pattern.

For my industry I could care less whether people went to college or not. That type of education isn't directly relevant to the situations a garage door technician faces on a daily basis. However, I like knowing someone graduated from college, because it shows they know how to see something through to the end. It takes years of hard work to get into college, earn a diploma, and pay for it. Anyone who has pulled that off should earn a few points in the recruiting process.

One of the biggest things I look for in new employees, of course, is a desire to help others win. I hire people who love to Elevate others. I want to hear interviewees talk about how they made big sacrifices in their lives because they wanted to make someone else proud, or pay kindness forward.

I also look for people who are passionate about something they do. I don't want to hire someone who talks casually about how everything is "pretty good" and they "don't have any complaints." That's boring. I like to hire people who have strong beliefs and take a stand about something.

One simple exercise is comparing how often a candidate says "I" versus "We." This can indicate whether someone is more of a team player or more self-centered. Make two columns on a page and tally up the mentions. What is the ratio of I's to We's? Is it greater than one or less than one?

With competitiveness being one of my core values, I want to see whether someone is a fighter before I hire them. And that's not something you can ask people straight out. Instead, I often challenge them during the interview and look to see whether they push back.

"I've got to be honest," I say, shaking my head, "I don't think you're cut out for a career with A1 Garage Door. I'm not sure you have what it takes." Then I shut up and see what they do. Will they put their tail between their legs and slink out of the office? Or will they stand up tall and fight back? I'm looking for them to say something like, "Hey, wait a minute, there's been a mistake here, because I'm the best. Give me the best guy. What are his numbers? If I can't match him, then fine, but try me first!"

But even if they give a perfect answer like this, I'll still keep pushing back on them—just to see how persistent they are.

"Oh, well, I don't know," I might say, crossing my arms sternly. "Now you're getting all worked up and emotional. But we need people who stay calm and level-headed." Again, do they back down and apologize or do they keep fighting?

"Call my last three references," they might demand. "I've been number one at every company I've worked for."

I've had this type of improv go back and forth quite a few times. If they fight back, it shows they are resilient and aren't pushovers. Of course, there's a fine line between confidence and a lack of social tact. You can see a lot about someone by throwing them into this type of situation.

Another thing I do sometimes during the interview process is sing a well-known song and ask the candidate to join me. For instance, this morning I went into "Happy Birthday" with a guy I was interviewing for an executive role. He hopped right in and sang with me, so I know he'll be a good fit. If someone lets me get through the song and doesn't even clap along, they don't have much spirit.

You can strangely tell a lot about someone's personality and what it will be like to work with them from my little singalong test. Some people will decline to sing along, but in nice ways. They might claim they feel sick or have a terrible voice. Then they often dance instead, or clap along. It's almost like they are making up for not singing with you. So, there are tactful ways to say no.

It undoubtedly seems funny not to hire someone simply because they wouldn't sing "Happy Birthday" with you, but it's a great way to see an applicant's personality. I use this test all the time, and teach it to my hiring people. I'm looking for employees who are serious and qualified, but also who know how to have fun. The singalong test helps me filter the wrong ones out.

Another simple thing you can usually do during an interview is role-play a typical interaction the candidate might have as part of the job they are going out for. If it's a veterinary clinic I'll pretend to call up, freaking out about my dog who slammed his leg in the door. And I'll see how effective they are at jumping into the situation, thinking on their feet, calming me down, and offering a plan to get my dog safely to the animal hospital. This type of exercise shows you more about a person in a few minutes than you could ever find out through lengthy questioning.

"We've got a major problem," I might say out of the blue during an interview, with a panicked look on my face. "We've got two calls on hold. One is an irate customer, who is super peeved. The other says her garage door opener never arrived in the mail. And you're on the phone with a third customer, trying to book a call. Then a fourth customer walked into the office, and they are at the front door waiting for you, tapping their foot. How do you handle the situation?"

It's helpful to surprise candidates with role-plays because you can see them think critically in real time. And it requires creativity. No two answers will be identical. Also, by presenting the scenario in a rushed way you can get their heart rate up and see how they perform under pressure.

Once again with this type of scenario you're also testing how willing they are to jump into an imaginary situation and play along with you. It's a similar idea to whether they will sing "Happy Birthday" with you or not. If they are too cool or shy to go for it, that's not a good sign.

Another key for interviewing is to put people into similar situations to what they will see on the job. So, if they are going to be in sales, see how well they build rapport with you. Do a role-play and see whether they can sell you something challenging. If someone is interviewing to be a CSR, all I care about is their phone voice. In this case, I don't even want to be distracted by what they look like, so I might talk to them on the phone for the interview. Similarly, when I'm interviewing a dispatcher, I like to put up three screens and see if they are good at solving puzzles, because that's a dispatcher's job. Get creative. How can you throw the candidate into imaginary situations that test skills you're interested in?

It works best to hire for mindset, rather than look for people with specific experience. I learned from Simon Sinek that it is better to hire for attitude rather than skills. Skills can be taught and it's easy to bring someone up to speed when you hire the perfect individual. It is much harder to turn somebody's attitude around if it doesn't sync with your philosophy and culture.

It's also not productive to make an interview too one-sided. You and the candidate are interviewing each other. Give them opportunities to see whether this is right for them or not, too. They should be asking questions about the company and feeling you out. You both should have some give and take with each other.

In addition to attitude, there are some technical skills you want to test during the interviews. These aren't necessarily deal breakers, but knowing the level of technical competency of your hires can greatly inform how you train them and save you hours of time. For example, screening candidates for basic computer literacy is something you shouldn't overlook on virtually any kind of interview these days. Adam

Cronenberg and I would ask them to copy and paste something to see if they were familiar with Ctrl C and Ctrl V. Then we'd ask them to open multiple windows in a browser.

While attitude is the main thing to look for in an operations-level employee, "culture fit" is a critical factor for managers and C-level people. In many ways, this phrase is often thrown around as an excuse to exclude people from an employment opportunity with no good reason. It can be used to write off people who don't fit the racial, political, or socioeconomic "vibe" of a company. And that's dangerous. On the other hand, it is a real concern in hiring people for the executive team that they must get along with your own personality and with the other people on your team. You don't want a clash.

I've discovered I'm a big idea guy, and I constantly spout off ideas. I need people around me who filter and execute on the ideas, not who throw a bunch of new ideas back at me. That creates chaos. This means I work well when I can collaborate closely on projects with co-workers who are more execution minded. That's important to know when we hire people for management positions.

What kind of personality do you have? Which types of team members would complement your team culture best? How can you be real about your requirements without being biased toward people who share a similar background?

Outside of the Regular Process

In today's world, you can uncover mountains of information about a candidate without even conducting an interview. Everyone's personal data is freely available online. But is it ethical to flip through the social media archives when you're considering someone for a position at your company? When does it cross the line?

For me, the main thing I'm trying to determine during interviews is what kind of attitude someone has. And it's fair to look through a candidate's social media photos for a general idea of their mindset. Do they smile? Are their posts depressing? Are they unhappy? Misery loves company. Unhappiness spreads like a disease. It's best not to hire unhappy people in the first place. They quickly infect others with their negativity. You know those people. They don't laugh frequently and find it difficult to have interesting conversations. They're not the best people to be around. You can feel the energy when people walk into the room. And I've found you can even feel it through pictures. Sometimes from a quick glance at a candidate's social media you get a bad vibe. It's fair to trust your gut in these situations. But make sure you're not using this as an excuse for bias.

The final trait to look for in all new hires is self-awareness. It's one of the most difficult traits to find and assess. How do you know whether someone is confident or cocky? Who are you to judge another person's level of self-awareness?

Sometimes you can learn a lot by asking people questions like, "What is your biggest weakness?" If they tell you something that's a strength, like "I work too hard" or "I'm too much of a perfectionist" or "I'm OCD and keep everything super organized," that doesn't demonstrate self-awareness. Those are good things, not weaknesses.

"Hi, I'm Tommy," a strong candidate might say, "and there are times when I haven't been self-motivated, so I didn't do as well with internet schooling as I did in the classroom. I like to be held accountable, which is why I have a personal trainer come to me for my health. Sometimes I take on too much and don't know how to prioritize correctly, so I work best with people who are good at keeping me on task. Everyone on my team knows how to pull me back on track when needed."

Look for people who demonstrate a profound understanding of their own tendencies, and who seem eager to consider ideas for how to correct their shortcomings. They should be open to your feedback and to brainstorming about how they can improve. You can feel it when someone has a high level of self-awareness. There's something indescribable about it.

You'll get better data on candidates if you pull them outside of the regular interview process. Do something unexpected. Get them responding to you as a real person. Break out of the usual interview script and get them relating to you as a human being. Go out for a few meals with someone so you can see what they are all about. This removes the focus on one single interview as the only chance to get the job. Chatting over a meal feels less formal than meeting in a conference room, so people are more likely to relax and open up.

I'll even take candidates with me on random trips around town sometimes. "Hey, Fernando," I'll say, grabbing someone right from the waiting room and heading out the door, "I'm swinging by the hardware store before they close to pick up a couple things. Come with me." And off we go to my car, the store, lunch, the dry cleaner, and back to the office.

When you only see someone for twenty minutes in the controlled setting of a conference room (or, worse yet, a Zoom call), you'll get one version of them. But if you jolt them out of the expected, you can see how they respond in real instances of uncertainty. Maybe someone can fake it for an hour during an air-conditioned interview with a hot cup of tea in their hand, but take them down to a smelly fish market in Chinatown, with guts flying through the air and buckets of eels stacked under foot, and their guard might slip.

Another point that also builds on the idea of getting candidates out of the office is to involve their significant others in the interview process. I was speaking at an event recently about recruiting and one interesting point that came out during our session was the importance of marketing your company to other decision makers in the candidate's household. The kind of great employees I'm looking for don't ever leave their companies. They work so hard it wouldn't be possible without support from their families and communities. Also, you get to see how they relate to one another. If you're unhappy at home, it's hard to be happy at work.

During the interview process I like to get the whole family on board. We bring the wives of the candidates in, along with a group of dynamic wives of current employees. They say things like, "Before he worked at A1 my husband wasn't a good dad, or husband. He wasn't appreciated at work. And he never had time off. But since moving to A1 Garage Door

Service, he's become a better man altogether. We're out of debt. We own a house. He's less stressed."

Instead of going after the individual directly, get someone they care about to advocate on your behalf. The type of value-driven employees you're looking for aren't necessarily going to quit their jobs for a chance to make more money. They are loyal. But their first allegiance is to their family. And if the kids and wife want them to get a new job, they will make the move.

There are two big topics when we talk about recruiting: C-suite and low- or mid-level personnel. The requirements on these types of workers are different, so we can't use the same approaches to recruit them. For C-suite people personality is critical because it's difficult for the company to grow if you have any animosity within your senior leadership team. At this level, there are things going on behind closed doors, and any obstacles can get in the way of growth. There must be high levels of trust, honesty, and transparency.

Also, you don't find C-suite people by posting on a regular job board somewhere. Instead, you recruit them. This means researching the type of people you want to work with, going to LinkedIn, and reaching out to them. You're looking for C-level candidates who have already been where you're trying to go as a company. You don't want them learning on your watch. Small companies don't get many chances to make big mistakes. If you can't afford a good high-end Chief Financial Officer (CFO), you might look into a fractional CFO. This is an experienced CFO who provides services for organizations on a part-time, retainer, or contractual agreement.

For lower-level people, on the other hand, the opposite approach makes the most sense. It's not realistic to fill every role with highly experienced people. You're better off hiring for attitude and watching closely to see who works out and who doesn't.

Another rabbit hole you can get sucked into with recruiting is negotiating starting salaries. My philosophy on negotiating has evolved over time. I used to work hard to wear people down to the lowest number possible. But that's draining and it doesn't kick the employment relationship off on the best foot. Why start with a battle?

These days, I've realized hard-nosed negotiation isn't necessary. This is especially true when you're dealing with A-players. The employees I'm looking for should be confident in their ability to perform above average. So, my strategy is to give them a healthy base salary that can cover essentials, and then tie the rest of their pay to performance. This setup appeals to winners because they like the idea they can earn more if they get better results. I believe people want to know they'll earn enough to pay for rent, gas, food, the car, the phone, and other basics. But beyond that, the best employees will jump at the chance to make their pay contingent on performance. It's a setup that makes sense for both sides.

Finding excellent employees is an art that takes time to master. There are so many things to keep track of during the interview process, it can seem daunting. But don't try to tackle everything at once.

To begin with, focus on three key attributes and forget everything else. If you have read *The Ideal Team Player* by Patrick Lencioni, then you already know that he says we should look for employees who are humble, hungry, and smart. When you think about it, it makes sense. If you find a candidate with those three qualities, they will be teachable, motivated, and they will fit into your culture. Remember those three words. They will serve you well.

Humble. Hungry. Smart.

Danny Kerr's Best Tips

It's been seventeen years since Danny had to make the tough decision whether to delay his clients while he recruited new painters or do the work himself. Since those early days he has conducted over 1,500 interviews leading to hundreds of hires for his growing organization. Today, he is the co-owner of Breakthrough Academy. He took what he learned from the school of hard knocks and now advises other entrepreneurs on how to improve all aspects of their businesses, so they don't repeat his early mistakes—especially their recruiting. I asked him for his best ideas on how to hire superstars, and his answers surprised me.

One of the first things Danny stressed is that you should spend time collecting data before making major changes to your hiring practices. The better you get at forecasting your needs into the future, the more you will crush recruiting, because it's easier to find the perfect person when you have advance notice. It's like leaving a fishing net out in the water for three minutes versus three days. You'll have a better chance of the right one coming along and getting caught if you can leave it out there longer.

Once you collect some data, Danny told me, use math to figure out who to hire next, not your emotions. It's not about "I feel like we should hire another project manager." Instead, the conversation is more like "One project manager equals $1.5 million in produced revenue. That means two salespeople at $750,000 in booked revenue each. With their overhead costs and bonus structures, we should make a fifteen percent margin. So, it makes sense to bring someone on, based on our current lead flow."

Once you have a couple years of data, you see how it's not a random guess. Numbers allow you to move strategically. So, if you aren't collecting data, start right away. You never know when it will come in handy down the line.

Danny believes that today's economy companies that are active with their hiring will beat out those that are passive. We can't expect great employees to find us on their own anymore. Passive strategies are ones that involve posting. Job boards like Indeed, ZipRecruiter, and Craigslist are all examples. Active strategies, on the other hand, are more like setting up a referral program kickoff with your team, where everyone messages 100 people. Active is sending 250 direct messages every day on LinkedIn, or holding all resumes from everyone to ever apply and remarketing to them for three years to see if they need a job later on.

Danny says his approach to recruiting is similar to how most people think about marketing. If you build a predictable funnel, you'll be okay. When Danny starts working with a new company on optimizing their recruiting, he first develops an ideal candidate profile. He wants to figure out who he is trying to attract. This informs the job description and marketing funnel, which drives traffic to a landing page where people can apply.

In Danny's world, everything throughout the recruiting process for a certain role is designed around a specific personality type. He is confirming multiple times along the way from application, to interview, to negotiation, to hiring, so that only the right kind of people continue on with the process.

Danny also uses every communication with applicants as an opportunity to set their expectations with regard to what's coming up in the process and what it will look like if they do, or don't, end up getting hired. It's a good idea to overly inform people about how the process works, and what steps are coming up next. They should never feel confused.

Don't sell people on a transactional employment relationship, says Danny, in which you give them money and they give you time in return. It should be bigger than that, he thinks. What keeps people around more than anything is if you're developing them and keeping them in a constant state of improvement. The right people love this. As long as they are moving forward, they're good. So, sell them on that from the beginning.

More than perks, people want the opportunity to grow. Promise them that and they will work hard for you. Danny noticed other recruiters pitching people on virtually the same perks (a better salary, nicer truck, cooler office, etc.). But their selling points were surface level and transactional. What he found attracted his highest performers was blunt yet constructive feedback. As he interviews them, Danny breaks down their past performance. He looks at their ability to set goals and handle stress, as well as their introspection, personality traits, and more. After an hour and a half of interviewing the candidates, he offers some feedback.

Danny tells applicants where they are strong, and which patterns in their stories back that assessment up, as well as where they are weak, and which patterns demonstrate that too. He explains that if the two of them were going to work together, they would develop a customized plan to best utilize the applicant's strengths and improve on their weaknesses. The best people get excited to see how much better they could get working with Danny for a while. But the weak people don't like hearing about themselves, and get defensive. From there it's easy to decide who to hire.

It's surprising that so few people study interviewing skills. Danny has found it's valuable to be good at this. Interviewing is about understanding the needs of another human being, listening to their stories, being able to relate to them, and reading between the lines. For most of us, interviewing is a low priority, which we squeeze in around everything else. But for Danny it has always been vital.

One thing Danny does right off the bat, to get people to drop their defenses, is he encourages them to be real. He likes to point out to candidates that nobody wants a job that's not right for them, so there's no point in being inauthentic.

"Tell me who you are," Danny says, "and I'll provide helpful feedback for you. And if it's a good fit I'll put you in a role where you're going to dominate and have fun. If it's not a good fit, I'll tell you why and give you some thoughts on what you could do to improve over time. Be real. We're together in this process."

It only takes about thirty seconds, and you can deliver the same script with every candidate. This simple little preface gets people to relax. It's also great to take a few deep breaths together with people before you start—if that's possible.

During the interview, Danny says, there's a huge difference between merely asking about something and truly going deep. You can ask whether the candidate is a hard worker, for example. Of course, they'll say, "Yeah!" So, that's not a helpful question. Instead, try asking a series of more specific questions:

- What's your hardest work experience?
- How long did it last?
- What was your hardest day? Hardest week?
- When did you want to quit?
- What were you thinking at the time?
- Why didn't you quit?
- What did you think about your boss?

It's also helpful to phrase your questions in a way that assumes the person is going to answer. For instance, Danny says he makes sure to say, "What was the biggest argument you ever had at work?" instead of, "Did you ever have a big argument at the office?" In the second case, they could say no. By phrasing it the first way, you're at least going to get some answer.

One recruiting situation Danny specifically mentioned to watch out for is when you're hiring a friend, family member, or someone you've known for a long time. Often, when this happens, we skip the interview process altogether. After all, we know this person is trustworthy. And maybe they are fully qualified. But even still, it's not a good idea to skip the interview process. In doing so, we overlook the fact that the process itself tends to set expectations. The candidate knows this is when you're supposed to question them, look into their past behavior, provide thoughts and feedback, and push back in areas where you want to see improvement. Set the expectation from the start of your relationship with a new employee that the job is not going to be a free ride. Make it clear they show promise, but you expect to see significant improvement.

Also, Danny is careful to refer to the "interview process" and never just to an "interview." Because it should be a process. Conduct multiple interviews. It's crazy that people will spend only twenty to forty minutes picking someone they are going to hire for two or four years. It's like speed dating followed by marriage. That might work on reality TV, but in real life, slow things down. Don't rush.

Recruiting isn't a quick box to tick off so you can get back to doing the real work. It is the real work. If you run any kind of service business, you manage labor. At a fundamental level that is the business you are in. You find talented people, hire them, train them, and manage them. So, your ability to do that efficiently will dictate your success. Can you attract, retain, and drive high-quality people? This skill will serve you well as we head into a world where the biggest asset in your company is, in his opinion, your people. This is especially true in the post COVID world where employees now have higher expectations for how their companies care for them.

* * *

A Message from Tommy Mello

Hey Reader,

Can you take a minute to do something important? Just like a technician should ask a customer to leave a review for them personally, I'm asking you to leave a review of this book as a favor to me.

Whether you're listening to the book on Audible, enjoying it on an e-reader, like a Kindle, or reading the print version, could you write a few words about your thoughts on this book and add a rating? Please, please, help me Elevate the industry and get this book into more people's hands. Just open your Audible App or visit Amazon.com and tell everyone what you think.

I much appreciate it,

Tommy Mello

P.S. Some of the most valuable friends in my life have been the ones who introduced me to new ways of thinking. If you blow someone's mind they will love and respect you forever. So, if you want a friend for life, send a copy of this book to an entrepreneur you know. Thank you from the bottom of my heart. Now, on to the next chapter!

As a way to thank you for taking the time to leave this review, I wanted to share some of my best resources that you can use to implement the ideas in this book.

Just go to **https://tommymello.com/elevatebook**

or

email us at **elevatebook@tommymello.com**

Chapter 6
The Fifth Pillar: Systems

SOMETHING REMARKABLE HAPPENED to the most abysmal cycling team on the planet, and the story reveals a profound truth about the role of systems within any organization.

It was 2008, and British Cycling wasn't merely terrible; they were possibly the worst professional bicycling organization in existence. Their rankings going into the Beijing Olympics were laughable. British riders had never won the Tour de France in 110 years and had only won a single Olympic gold medal during that same time. One leading U.K. bicycle manufacturer even forbade the team from riding their bikes in public, worried it could tarnish the company's good image. But somehow at the Olympic games that year this rag-team team of write-offs won in an astronomical landslide, taking gold medals in sixty percent of the events they competed in. Then they did the same thing again in London four years later. And they won the Tour de France, too, not once, or twice, but five times during the following six-year stretch.

Many critics consider this the most impressive run by any cycling team in recorded history, which is difficult to comprehend since they'd been widely written off as laughable by the cycling world prior to the start of the Beijing Olympic games. So, what happened in China? How did everything change so fast?

The story begins five years earlier, in 2003. That's when British Cycling, also known as Team Sky, hired a new coach, Dave Brailsford, and he made small changes to the way the team did things. Nothing was drastic, but there was one major shift. Instead of blaming the team for their performance, David insisted on blaming the processes. His philosophy, which he called "the aggregation of marginal gains," was all about doing things the same way every time, and constantly experimenting with small tweaks to yield a one percent improvement. Eventually, this added up to a big difference. When enough of these little improvements are stacked on top of each other, the combined result is huge.

Since the cyclists of Team Sky were on the road all the time, they had trouble getting good sleep. This affected their performance by at least a few seconds. What could they do to sleep better? The team reached out to the Moscow Ballet and talked with the ballerinas, who often had to sleep on the road while performing in big shows. The ladies said their best advice was to travel with a pillow. So, the bikers did that, and their sleep improved some.

Another big problem that the cyclists faced was getting sick. Since the team spent time together in close locker rooms and buses, bacteria spread through the group in a matter of days, infecting everyone. So, Brailsford hired a doctor to develop a plan for keeping everybody healthy. One thing the doctor did was train the team to wash their hands like surgeons. The athletes agreed to avoid shaking hands at all for a few days before big races, to minimize the chances of an infection while riding.

Also, standing around waiting for races to start was slowing the team down. During that time, their leg muscles got cold. Once the race finally got underway, it took the riders a moment to get warmed up again (especially on cold days). To fix this, the team wore heated shorts to keep their legs warmed up to the perfect temperature until just before the race began. That helped.

None of these changes, on their own, made a huge difference. Most of the time the results were hardly noticeable, usually less than one percent. But for some reason Brailsford, undeterred, pressed on. He tweaked the seat design and used biofeedback technology to determine which workout and massage gel each athlete responded to best. He tested new experimental fabrics for their uniforms, protected the bikes from dust particles during transit, and made hundreds more tiny little adjustments.

The results didn't show up right away, but David's patience was rewarded in Beijing. After five long years of gradually stacking these tiny changes on top of each other, the overall effect was massive. British Cycling went from one of the worst teams ever to one of the best. While the transformation may appear rapid from the outside, it was slow and determined from within.

Like Coach Brailsford, we all can massively improve our businesses, families, and organizations by developing systems and working to refine them one change at a time. These improvements can add up to a big shift. But before it works, we must set detailed systems which will help us improve.

If a ten-year-old B-student can't come into your office and learn a process within an hour, then the process failed, and your training failed. Go back and make it simpler. Always blame the process, never the people. Managers often complain about how their employees are incompetent and can't do things right. This is funny to me, because it shows the manager is incompetent, not the worker. The manager is responsible for maintaining the procedures and manuals. So, if a process is unclear and difficult to follow, we should fix the protocols, not complain about employees.

If you're like me, you're efficient at most things you do because you have systems. You've developed routines to get your laundry done, buy groceries, exercise, shower, eat, work, and socialize. You've refined your systems for years without realizing it. You can use calculators, spreadsheets, and keyboard shortcuts (like copy and paste). Without these processes it would be tough to do even basic things.

It's not that you and I are smarter or better than people who don't have these systems. In fact, many other people have learned systems that you and I would find foreign. For instance, star NFL wide receiver Larry Fitzgerald, Jr. has run the same routes so many times that he can go ten feet then break. He will never accidentally run eight feet or twelve. When he steps on the field during a game he doesn't think about his route because he's practiced it so many times.

The systems we implement in business must be simple. Otherwise, people get frustrated and stop using them. Create checklists to keep things organized and introduce accountability. Break complicated processes down into smaller steps, and break each of those into sub-steps. One process might have eight steps, each with ten sub-steps. So, there are eighty things to complete and check off before the process is complete. But each individual step is simple. All a worker ever has to do is complete one step, check it off, and move on to the next one.

In many ways, the business world is similar to the army, where soldiers must take out their guns and put them together blindfolded in twenty seconds flat, with a drill sergeant screaming. We want our people to know the systems within our company cold. Whatever tasks someone is responsible for should have agreed-upon protocols that employees are trained to follow.

"Imagine I put you in the middle of a major league baseball field," I said the other day during a training session, "on the pitcher's mound, during the middle of a World Series game. I want you to recite to me, without hesitating, how to sell someone a new garage door. I want to know the words to use, when I should smile, what steps to follow, and how to make the offer."

When my trained technicians step into a garage, everything needs to come back to them. All those drills, role-plays, and scripts were practice to get people ready for the game. When it's finally gametime, I don't want them consciously thinking about all the practice. I want them to let it go and trust they can deliver when it counts. The amazing trainers at A1 have done their job. Now they need to do theirs.

The secret to performance under pressure is to practice with the systems. Anyone who has to execute their duties in extremely high-stakes situations usually drills every possible scenario repeatedly, until they know what to do subconsciously. That's my philosophy with our technicians, too, because I want them to all be at that level of preparation. I want to blindfold them, spin them around, and have them recite it all back to me, perfectly.

My journey with developing and refining systems for employees at my company started over a decade ago, on the day I first decided to hire an assistant. I felt if I wanted her to do everything properly (meaning, how I would do it), I needed to spell it all out and put in the time to train her. Eventually, I created a guidebook for her to follow, with descriptions, warnings, and templates for anything she could possibly encounter as part of her job. I spent months going through my inbox and making voice memos about every person who emailed me. I wrote down notes on who people are, how long I've known them, and what we are working on together. This helped with passing responsibilities over to my first assistant. Then I put her in charge of maintaining the guidebook, keeping it updated, and passing it along to the next assistant after her. I don't want to spend six months training a new person whenever someone leaves. Creating systems and guidebooks helps me avoid that.

As a company gets bigger, the jobs of the CEO and COO revolve increasingly around systems. You're looking at the current systems and finding ways to make things work more smoothly. The larger an organization gets, the more systematized everything must be to function properly. And, you're constantly refining old systems and adding new ones.

I develop new systems all the time. I'm working on one now. The other day I went to Leland Smith's company, Service Champions, and I saw they have a one-hour tune-up. These guys install and maintain A/C units. And they can spend a full hour tuning up one of those little boxes! I was amazed at the number of detailed systems they have developed to legitimately spend that long tuning up an air conditioner.

"I want a 1-hour garage door tune-up," I said yesterday to my head service technician as I walked through the factory. "Let's make this happen!"

"Hey, wait a minute," he protested. "What are you talking about? How do you expect me to do that? It's impossible to spend that long tuning up a garage door."

"I honestly don't know," I said. "But I'm confident you'll come up with something phenomenal. Remove the case from the opener. Take pictures of everything and send them through the client portal for review. Rewire every wire. Add self-tappers onto every single thing. Come up with an 80-point tune-up that has a picture on every screen. I know you're going to build something special. You're a superstar, and that's why I'm giving this important task to you."

He nodded.

"I need this by Friday," I finished, and walked away before he could protest any further. They're working on it as I write this, and from what I hear it should be on track for a demonstration in a few days. This is going to be a massive improvement over the quick tune-ups we've been doing. When we walk into your garage with a 151-point tune-up and send you pictures of everything we're doing, that builds trust. It's a way of adding value. Whereas if we walk into the garage for a couple of minutes, peek at the opener, and say everything looks good, that doesn't feel nearly as valuable.

Service businesses follow this simple formula:
Time = Value

That's why our new motto when our techs are out in a customer garage doing an inspection is How Slow Can You Go? I want them to follow our systems carefully. No cutting corners. It's not about racing through to the end; it's about being meticulous with everything we do.

Anyway, the point is the team and I are constantly working to develop new systems to improve all aspects of our business here at A1, and you should be doing the same at your company. Also, be willing to get your top team members involved in events, visiting other shops and giving them opportunities to be hungry for knowledge. Be open to learning from what others are doing.

Systems for Onboarding

You need good systems for onboarding. Your company is going to grow a lot in the near future, and that means onboarding many new employees. Things you do frequently should be systematized. Let's think about what better onboarding systems might look like for your company.

It's easy to overlook onboarding as a formality and not spend much time on it. Why not copy what other companies are doing? Then you can move on.

The time when new employees are busy forming their first impressions of their workplace is critically important. Why throw that opportunity away or leave it up to chance? You can never recover from making a bad first impression on a new employee. When they show up for their first day, that initial impression is everything.

Here at A1 we want to wow new hires right off the bat, and that's important to us. We want to Elevate them and treat them like winners right from the beginning. We never want to waste their time or make them feel undervalued. As a result, we've developed a set of specific systems for onboarding every new co-worker.

You may already have onboarding systems in place. Either way, there is always room for improvement. Ask yourself how you can be overly thoughtful and achieve a "WOW" reaction from new employees during their first week. When your new hires show up for their first day is the front desk ready to rock and roll? Is their workstation set up for them? If they are a CSR, do they have a headset and a computer? If they are a technician, do they have gear and a locker? Do they have eye protection, the books we hand out, and a scheduled plan of their orientation from Tommy?

We give people a lot on their first day of work. But it's not random crap. It's a carefully curated welcome package we've been crafting for years. We give them books to read, a swag mug, t-shirt, notepad, and all kinds of A1 memorabilia. Their agenda for the first week is printed out on their desk, with their name on the page and today's date. Their new hire paperwork is also nicely printed and fully pre-populated with the information we have on file for them, as a convenience.

Do you take people to lunch on their first day and spend time getting to know them on a personal level? If not, you should. It goes a long way.

Get their attention with an orientation that's outside of the box. Sitting in a room watching videos and PowerPoint talks is not the most inspiring thing. What can you do to break their expectations, get their heart rates up, and get their adrenaline pumping? The more memorable, the better. It sets the tone for their time with your company.

A positive first impression can keep a relationship strong even if everything isn't perfect down the line. It sets a solid foundation and gives you something to fall back on during hard times.

Also, this phase is an opportunity to prevent future misunderstandings by clarifying everything with new hires upfront before getting started. Let people know the expectations, and how to win, starting from their first day.

"Here's the exact playbook on working for Tommy Mello," I tell people during training. "The great news about me is that I'm going to give you freedom to solve problems however you want and to prioritize what's most important. I'm not going to micromanage you or tell you how to do your job. I'm going to expect you to make good decisions, because you're an adult and I want to treat you that way. If there's a problem, come to me with a solution to pitch. Don't come with problems. Do research and present me with a simple opportunity to make an informed choice."

I've found people appreciate this frank and transparent approach. They like knowing what I want so they don't have to guess. I also let people know what the specific expectations are for each project, quarter, or year.

Even with the work we've done building systems here at A1, there is always more to do. We're frequently discovering new things to add and holes to patch. For instance, we have a new video guy who started this month. During his first week, he already made us realize we need to create about ten critical systems and manuals, because he asked the right questions.

We requested that our new video guy come on a trip and film the whole thing for social media. It seemed basic. Come with us, bring a camera, point it, and press the button. But he had questions. And they were good things to ask.

- How do I get paid while I'm traveling, is there an overtime rate for that?

- Or am I getting paid for every hour I'm gone, like I'm working 24 hours a day?
- And what about my meals, will we eat together? Or, if we eat on our own, is Tommy covering those, or do I pay for them myself?
- And for the flights and hotels and everything, am I paying for the ticket myself and getting reimbursed, or do you set that up on your end, or what?
- What camera equipment can I check out from the company to take on the trip? How does that work and how do I sign up to take something out?
- What happens if a piece of equipment breaks while we are on location somewhere?
- How do I submit a form if I need the company to purchase a new piece of equipment?

We learned a lot from this kid, and realized we needed to create new systems as a result. It's been astonishing to see how many processes we've developed to Elevate our people at A1, and it's humbling to think about everything that is still left to build. While the processes are polished for hiring techs and CSRs, it's a different story for a full-time videographer. We've never hired one of those before. Everything is new for this role.

As you hire more people and put them into your system, look for the questions they ask and the concerns they share. These are sticking points you can potentially smooth out. Provide explanations in advance. Make things clearer. Break big ideas into smaller ones. Take special note of new employees' questions and concerns. Try to foresee questions ahead of time and answer them in advance. Put yourself into the employees' shoes and imagine what is going to be scary, confusing, or unclear for them. Then address those things.

- How do they get it cleared when they want to take vacation?
- How can they expense purchases?
- What should they do if an emergency happens?

- Do they get health and retirement benefits as part of their compensation package?
- Is there any performance pay ever tied to this role? If so, when does it start and how do they earn it?

When these types of basic questions aren't addressed during onboarding and training, it can be awkward. People get confused, but they don't know where to go for help. In other words, we failed to properly prepare them for the obstacles that were going to come their way in the course of doing their jobs. That's an error on behalf of the entrepreneur.

Think about everything that could go wrong, develop processes for how to handle each scenario, and write those down into a practical guide for employees. Then train them on how to implement the procedures you've written down in the guidebook. Your employees should feel like the military trainee who can take his gun apart and put it back together in the dark, in complete silence, in less than twenty seconds. Writing the guide isn't enough. Make sure your employees know it front to back.

Think about how you can set your people up for success. Giving them the processes to deal with every issue they could face is a great way to do that. Then it comes down to training.

Systems for Training Employees

Learning systems is generally boring. So how do you get your employees to care and pay attention while you're training them?

Design your systems around the principle of "What's In It for Me." It's one of the basic laws of human behavior. We don't take actions in this world that aren't helping us or our close kin. Keep this in mind and remind your employees how the systems benefit them. The systems are here to Elevate employees and help them win. Your training should promise specific benefits that employees want. Tell them what's in it for them.

Your instruction also must be specific. You can't tell somebody to go out and make sales. Break each process down into steps and sub steps, with lessons, demonstrations, templates, and examples. Then train each employee on how to do it all. In detail. This isn't something where you break a sales call into ten steps, walk through each one for a few minutes, and set people free to try it on their own. It needs to be more like seventy steps. Teach them where to stand, where to park, when to smile, and what to say. This also includes tone, body language, and even the way they shake your hand, which create over ninety percent of the sales. Practice, recite, role-play, ride-along, and repeat until they know what to do in any situation, almost like it's second nature.

Training is a separate category from onboarding because you need both. While you only onboard employees once when they first begin working with your company, you train all your employees forever. Training is not something people eventually graduate from. It doesn't end, even when people get the word "senior" added to their titles. It should be continuous and ongoing.

Could you ever imagine a top athlete or performer who stopped training because they felt like they couldn't possibly get any better? People who are the best in the world at something spend more time training than anyone else. So why wouldn't we expect the same for our employees? If we want them to be great, we have to train them—and keep training them.

Training is an ongoing process that never ends. Nobody should ever consider themselves to be "fully trained." We always have more to learn. I'm the CEO and I'm constantly attending conferences, seminars, workshops, and coaching sessions. I can't tell you how many different consultants and performance coaches I work with. So, if I'm at the top of the organization and I'm not done with my training, nobody else should be either.

One department where training is extremely important is sales. Having the right systems in place for people to follow is critical for the success of your sales team. Small tweaks to the process can make big differences in closing ratios. This is why salespeople are known for recording and analyzing videos of their calls.

There is a tendency among salespeople to rely on natural ability and the "gift of gab," but this is a mistake. Some sellers tell me they can't follow a script too closely because they don't want to seem inauthentic during their interactions. And, besides, don't you want to be fully present with the prospect and respond to them in real time? If you're closely following a plan for the conversation, and then the prospect goes off script, how do you deal with that? Maybe it's better to never use the script to begin with?

While there is certainly room on every sales call for chatting with the prospect and building rapport, the bulk of the interaction should be scripted. Legendary sales trainer and author, Tom Hopkins, talks about "repeating the way that I do it. Don't make it your own until you've mastered the way I do it." By systematizing every detail and testing out different things at our training center we've been able to discover thousands of tiny tweaks to the process that all improve outcomes. This has allowed us to vastly improve the results of our sales team overall.

For instance, when our techs show the customer how their garage door works, we get down on one knee and look up at them in a specific way, to make them feel empowered. We teach that to our techs during training. We've noticed the picture you send to the customer matters, too. You've got to be smiling, and it's best if it's one with your family in it. We also show our people how to do pre-work before an appointment, like looking the house up and seeing when it last sold, finding the person on Facebook and LinkedIn, and listening to their initial booking call to put together a plan.

We also train people on less specific things they can do to be good representatives of the A1 brand out in the community. I tell my guys not to worry about the pricing. I already figured out the pricing to be high enough that they can always choose to do right by the customer. So, whenever there is any way they can be helpful to the customer, I want them to do it with a smile.

"Treat everyone like your mom," I tell my guys, "and watch what happens."

If mom needs help getting her Christmas lights taken down, you help her out because it's the right thing to do. If a tech is over at a customer's house and it's an old lady who is worried about how she's going to take down her Christmas lights, what should he do? Get up on that ladder! One tech recently did an appointment with an elderly couple who hadn't driven for quite some time. Both of their car batteries were dead. Our guy, Justin, ended up spending two hours jumping both of their cars. Isn't that what you'd do for mom? I was so proud to hear that story. Think of the positive word of mouth spreading around the community when we have 400 guys out there on the road every day treating their customers like that.

Training might not seem sexy or exciting, but it's one of the biggest things limiting most entrepreneurs from scaling their companies. Sometimes business owners train everyone themselves, which creates a massive bottleneck. Or, frequently, small companies don't even have formalized training. Instead, they rely on hiring people with prior experience.

Sometimes what seems to be a hiring problem, or a sales problem, or a quality control problem, is a training issue. If you had better training, then hiring wouldn't be so hard because you could focus on attitude rather than skills. If you prepared your salespeople better, they would close more deals. If you had clearer installation guidelines, quality would be simpler to maintain. When I played football, we used to practice five or six days a week, working out twice a day. Sometimes we practiced twelve days to play one single game. It might seem boring to have manual standard operating procedures and checklists. It's not exciting. It's vanilla. But if you get good at the vanilla things, the business begins to become easier to grow and scale.

When the full system in this book is all working together, the five pillars all feed into each other continuously. The pieces fit together and the whole thing churns smoothly under the hood, like a luxury car. For instance, the way you conduct your training sets the tone for the culture at your company. It also influences your recruiting. And it even feeds back into your marketing.

One example of the pillars working together in perfect harmony happened the other day. We did an exercise during a training workshop where we passed out dart guns to everyone and had them competing to shoot darts at different targets. Our social media guy there to film the whole thing and put it online. I was walking around our training facility while the team all shot darts at each other, having a great time, and it hit me how everything came together in this one moment. Our recruiting pillar found this group of people, and passed them into the training pillar, where they were experiencing the culture pillar and becoming a part of the marketing pillar. And none of it could happen without strong leadership.

Take a moment to imagine you live in my area and work at a competing garage door company. You're scrolling through social media tonight and come across this video showing how much fun we have during our training over here at A1. Or maybe you are a superstar garage door tech who recently moved to Phoenix from the east coast. You are considering jobs with different companies but haven't figured out where you want to land. Then you pull up your feed and see that video.

Systems for Accountability and Performance

The final type of system your company needs relates to monitoring each employee's performance and giving them feedback on their productivity. How do you make sure everyone gets enough done and it's all up to company standards? Managers can't spend all their time checking in on workers. How can you set simple checks and balances to reward employees who go the extra mile without creating extra work?

One simple example of checks and balances comes from my world, the garage door business. In this industry, each technician has a truck along with parts, equipment, and tools. Techs are supposed to inventory their trucks each morning and carefully stock them with everything they might need. This is important because it's a huge setback to get into the field and realize they are missing some critical piece, or forgot to charge a necessary tool.

Techs use checklists to prepare their trucks each morning. But it would take forever for managers to come through every day and make sure the trucks are all properly stocked. So, instead, once per week we have a single quiz where the manager randomly checks seven items.

And if they are all good, you pass. And if not, you get a small corrective write-up. We also have dispatchers look at the trucks before dispatching.

That reminds me, corrective write-ups are another system to create within your company. How do you discipline employees who don't follow the rules? Or who don't hit their numbers? Set up processes for dealing with problem employees and, if necessary, removing them from the company. Do people have three strikes before you'll let them go? What counts as a strike? It's a mistake to wait until something goes wrong to realize you never set these things up. Create a system for corrective write-ups from the beginning, and make sure employees learn it during onboarding. There's only one thing we don't tolerate at A1, and that's if you lie, cheat, or steal.

Don't turn into a rigid dictator with strict systems for everything, but do set up checks and balances to make sure everyone does their jobs properly. Some of the biggest mistakes I ever made in business were hiring the wrong people and allowing them to hold a blanket over my eyes. I kept them around too long. Everyone is going to make mistakes with hiring. That's impossible to avoid. But with good accountability systems you can catch those issues earlier and correct them. So, make sure you not only have the perfect CFO, but also the right CPA keeping an eye on the CFO.

Accountability is something we can build into every system. Any time I'm implementing a new system at A1, I spend time thinking about how to ensure people follow the procedures. But it's not easy to figure out how to collect data and enforce accountability. When systems are new, keep an eye out for ways people might bend the rules. Make tweaks until you get rid of the loopholes.

Many people want to work from home these days, and it's a huge perk if you can let them. It opens the door for great employees who want to work, but are also trying to raise kids, or who live far away from your offices. Of course, remote work makes more sense for certain positions and types of work than others. But either way, you need good systems in place to make sure people are productive while working remotely. Most employees get more done when they go into the office. But a funny thing happens where we convince ourselves we work better from home. So, collect data and show people if their productivity is not where it needs to be. Then look at solutions.

Performance pay is one of the most important accountability systems to set up in any business. But there are big mistakes people make when they first get started with it. If you set this up wrong, performance pay can be a disaster. You might start too low, which could insult employees rather than motivating them. Or you could go too high, in which case the program will drain your bank account and you'll be forced to go back on it.

Never start someone out on any kind of performance pay unless you have at least three months of previous data to see how much they would have earned.

I made a big mistake with performance pay one time, and it cost us a fortune. It happened when we decided to give trainers a bonus depending on how their recruits performed. At the time, this seemed like a good idea. It would motivate trainers to work harder and prepare their people better. What could go wrong?

Adam and I were sitting on the couch going through some numbers one evening after work. "Hey," I said, "why don't we give our trainers an extra bonus depending on how their students do in the first few months after training?"

"Yeah!" Adam was enthusiastic. "That's an awesome idea. We could either give them an extra $500, $1,000, or $1,500 depending on how well the recruit does during their first ninety days."

"Genius!" I said.

Except, as I thought about this brilliant plan over the coming days, I realized it would never work. We were training thirty technicians every month at the time. We'd need to rebuild the training center, hire nine more trainers and five recruiters. This could add up to over $400,000 per year in extra costs easily. And would it make much of a difference in the quality of the training? Not likely.

The moral of the story is when you give an offer for performance pay, you need historical data. Don't ever give an offer based on speculation.

This isn't a system to come up with off the top of your head. It should be based on data.

Setting the Systems Loose

Creating and maintaining systems can get exhausting. As your company scales and you put new processes into place, overseeing them all can become your full-time job. Eventually, you must pass responsibility off to others. Today, it's increasingly possible to automate systems. But, still, someone must manage the machines at the end of the day.

One helpful tip is to involve the people you ultimately want to pass the system over to in the process of developing it. Then they'll feel a sense of ownership from the beginning. Also, if you get the right people involved in writing procedures and manuals for each department, the guides will end up balanced and thoughtful. One of the best ways to get people to buy into anything is to have them help you build it, so getting employees to write the rulebook is a great idea. At one point early on we were making decisions about appearance and accessories for our staff. We had meetings about the rules. People voted on what they thought was most fair. And the employees decided, on their own, we don't want visible tattoos for people who work with customers. They also decided beards would be ok as long as they were trimmed.

Today in my company the manuals for every department are actively maintained by the employees within that department. I haven't written one for years, but they are perfectly up to date. Whenever an employee has a suggestion to improve their department's manual, they follow the process to submit a suggestion, which is reviewed by the team and voted on. So, the guidebooks maintain themselves at this point. And we laid the foundation for that years ago by including employees in the process of developing those procedures from the beginning.

At A1, each person has to read the manual, word by word and out loud. They also revisit the pages when necessary. For example, when everyone is getting ready for Thanksgiving and Christmas, they go into a meeting to read out loud the two pages that discuss how to take time off and how PTO (Paid Time Off) works. After all, we can't have everyone taking off Christmas vacation.

The top entrepreneurs in the world understand how important their time is and find ways to maximize it. I entered into a challenge recently. I made a bet that I could personally message every employee with a birthday, anniversary, or other notable event, and answer everything that happened on social media for the week in under an hour. Many people thought it was impossible. I got it all done in twenty minutes and won the bet. And now I've kept doing it every week because it's such an efficient system.

How it works is I have my people do all the hard work for me as preparation. They summarize each question or comment from social media into simple wording, so I can understand what the person wants from a glance. Then they pre-write responses for me, with cheat notes for what to say, but not exact words. When I step into my office everything is pulled up on my computer, in chronological order, with titles and descriptions pre-filled. All I do is record each one as a separate video file and upload the group to a cloud folder.

For every system you create within the company to make things more efficient for your employees, you can also look for places to automate work away. We live in a world of machine learning. There are automated solutions for many basic knowledge tasks you could think of having people do. And they are scary good. Remember that Elon Musk has the same amount of time as us, only twenty-four hours. There's no amount of money that could buy an extra minute so make it as efficient as possible.

One example of using automation to save work happened recently with a big contract. For some reason they wanted us to manually reach out to these homeowners to coordinate everything. We would need twenty more people for that. Instead, we got a system set up where ten minutes after a new homeowner signs up, it sends them a series of automated text messages to get the required information from them. And it asks them questions as needed, for additional clarification.

We automate so many things at my company, it's crazy. I tell people, "We're not a garage door company. We're a technology company that happens to sell garage doors." Automation can sometimes save you from having to recruit new employees. Maybe instead of hiring five junior people in your accounting department, you can hire one great person and automate everything else. There are even AI tools that will reconcile your bank account balance automatically.

Automation isn't about getting rid of human beings. It's about living in the world of exponential growth. And that's a fun world for your business to be in. The more things you can automate, the faster your company will grow.

Our users are currently scheduling ten percent of their calls automatically through a plugin called Schedule Engine. The goal is to get up to forty percent of all calls. This will significantly reduce the workload on our customer service representatives. The level of impact a single piece of software can make today is insane.

Systems are not infallible, and there are times you need to reevaluate them and make changes. When a system needs to be fixed, you may have to make decisions outside the system. Once I was in a meeting with our HR director and I learned our HR department was waiting on sending out an offer letter to a great candidate because his drug test hadn't come back yet.

"Well, shoot," I said, "can't we send it conditionally and say he's got the job as long as he passes the drug test? We don't want to lose him!"

We ended up getting that guy hired and he's been an exceptional employee. Months later, he told me he'd been about to accept another offer when ours came in. If we had waited another day waiting for the results, it would have been too late. I rub that in whenever I see our HR director. And now we send the offers as fast as we can. It matters.

A friend of mine went with his wife to visit her father's grave. At that point they had been married for ten years but my friend had never met her father because he'd died before they started dating. He said it felt weird going to his grave. When there, he noticed that next to where the dad was buried there was an empty plot.

"Who is going to get buried there?" he asked.

"Well, it was supposed to be my mom," she shrugged. "But since she's remarried now, it's kind of awkward."

Whoops.

Things change. Often in life and business we make decisions as if everything is going to stay the same forever, but that's a fantasy. Nothing ever stays the same. Change is the only true constant in the universe. Think about how your systems should stay updated and in step with the times, otherwise they will quickly become antiquated.

Ryan Mecham's Best Tips

One person who has helped me with improving the systems in my business more than perhaps anyone else is Ryan Mecham. He's a consultant who specializes in guiding companies to make the small changes that yield massive results. So, I asked him to share a few of his best ideas about how to improve systems in a business. One thing he told me was the story of Team Sky and British Cycling mentioned at the beginning of this chapter and the lesson about the importance of making small one percent gains.

For a company to have any kind of real, lasting success, Ryan says, you need a problem- solving process system that captures problems and ideas, then follows through and executes those ideas. You're looking for the compounding effect of the one percent improvements, like in the story of Team Sky. Coach Brailsford made small adjustments to the team's equipment, training, and uniforms, and his efforts ultimately led to a big difference.

Improving your systems isn't about becoming more efficient so you can get rid of employees, it's about empowering employees to spend their time doing things that add even more value. It ultimately impacts the customer. The idea, Ryan says, "is to identify the single biggest problem in your business and focus on making tiny incremental gains toward a solution. Those will gradually compound on top of each other into something meaningful."

Ryan helped me with this in my own business. He is a master at systematizing processes and improving by one percent at a time. For example, we have a division where we make custom garage doors, and it was not as profitable as it should have been. Ryan took a look and recognized the process involved too many people working together and too much variability.

We had three people who were each doing about a third of the work to produce one garage door. Ryan helped put new steps into action around the handoffs. Now the workers share a more level load and the whole thing runs smoother. Also, in the new system each worker must check a box to certify that everything looks good, so there is quality control at each step.

Many of the best ideas around how to improve our processes at A1 come from our employees. Every company needs a system for taking ideas from employees and customers and putting them into action. In home services, you usually have a five-to-fifteen-minute huddle with your team each morning in front of the white board. That's when you discuss safety, quality, throughput, and improvement ideas. Anybody with a suggestion can submit it at that time. Then the team will rate the ideas on a quadrant, with the two axes representing effort and impact. And they will look for the one that offers the best impact with the least effort. Every day you can try to implement a new idea, looking to make those little one percent gains anywhere possible.

"Whenever something goes wrong," says Ryan, "we shouldn't blame people and ask who messed up. Instead, we should look at what's wrong with the process, and ask how it allowed this error to happen." Toyota became the most profitable automobile company on the planet long before they were the largest. They made three times more profit than Ford, even though they were smaller. That's because they asked, "What in the process allowed this to happen?" rather than "Who let this happen?"

Toyota had multiple factories across Japan, and at every single one they made tens of thousands of tiny improvements in the process each year. They kept this up for years on end. Those changes gradually built on top of each other until they added up to something huge. That's how they got so good. It wasn't any single genius innovation.

At one company where Ryan worked as COO, a typical product initially took three weeks to make. After they implemented this methodology, the exact same product (with fewer people) took only forty-five minutes to produce. They also made a custom product, which took ten weeks to produce at first. But they got it down to five days from sale, to design, to manufacture, to shipping.

"Every company comes down to processes and people," Ryan says. That's what you have at the end of the day. But in most home services companies the processes aren't clear. You might have three technicians who all install a garage door differently. But now they can't learn from each other, and there's no agreed upon best practice. Also, if there's a customer complaint, it's difficult to respond. We don't know which method was used to install the door or what might be wrong. This makes more work for whoever's job it is to fix those things. The three techs must agree on the best installation process. When someone wants a new garage door, everyone at A1 has to be on the same page about which steps to follow. Then if anybody finds a way to improve the process by one percent, we can update it for everybody.

Systematizing your protocols into a manual shortens how long it takes for someone new to come into the business and get up to speed. New employees will have all the checklists, processes, and procedures right there for everything. That way they can see the recommended company approach for handling any situation. And this is better than relying on people to teach things to each other, because they might teach it wrong.

Some companies might assign new employees to shadow Johnny for their first week, because he's their best guy. But is Johnny using the best process? Is his success repeatable? Maybe Johnny is getting lucky. Maybe what works for him isn't best for the majority of people.

"Don't leave it up to chance that your people get trained properly," says Ryan. "Agree upon the best way of doing each task across the board. And if you find a one percent improvement, train everyone else to the new standard." We make work easier by creating processes and continuously improving those processes. Ryan also taught us to reward employees for finding errors in the day to day. That way they'll feel incentivized to help improve the processes in your company.

One word of caution, Ryan warns, is that as a company scales, the number of relationships goes up exponentially. For instance, when you go from two to four employees the total number of relationships only increases from one to six. However, when you move from four to eight employees the number of relationships goes from six to twenty-eight. It gets complicated fast. This is another reason to have systems and standards. What is simple now may soon be complicated. So, build the systems while you can, and improve them by one percent.

"Success in business," Ryan says, "is all about people and systems." And those are not incompatible ideas. In fact, they depend on and support each other perfectly.

Chapter 7
Getting Started

NOW YOU KNOW MY BUSINESS PHILOSOPHY, but there's one final idea to understand before you're ready to get out there and apply this in the real world. This final concept will help you put everything else together. When I realized this, my company took off, and it's one of the biggest things I share with other business owners. But it's one of the hardest things to convince people about, for some reason. That's what I struggled with a couple of years ago, when I spoke to a group of CEOs who all run garage door companies.

"A garage door opener costs about $1,500," I said, squinting through the bright lights into the room of entrepreneurs. "Who here is charging $10,500 to install one of those?" Silence. "Anybody?" I prodded. They all looked around. I was the only one raising my hand.

"Ok, fine," I relented. "Anybody charging $9,000?" No response. "What about $7,500?"

"That's a rip off," someone finally said, breaking the awkward silence.

"We can't take advantage like that," came another voice.

All around the room there were grunts of approval. Clearly everyone was in agreement that it isn't right to install a garage door opener for significantly more than it costs to buy the parts.

"Alright," I asked. "Well, who here has a brand new vehicle for all their employees?"

Again, no hands went up, except for my own.

"Who here trains the guys for eight weeks before they go out on a single call," I continued. "Or flies them all to the same city to attend workshops together? Who here offers paid time off, bonuses for good performance, and the best customer management software in the industry? Who here can afford sixty billboards in today's market?"

Shouts of dissent popped up from different corners of the room.

"There's no way we could afford all that," one man said angrily.

"You're crazy," mumbled a prickly fellow in the front row.

"I don't know how anyone could pay for that," said the soft-spoken man behind him.

"So, you mean to tell me," I paused, "that you screw over your employees to take care of your customers?" That shut them up. "You intentionally pay your people like crap," I continued, "hold their faces to the ground, and make sure they can't get ahead in life, or put their kids in private school, or go on their dream vacation? All so you can take care of your customers?"

"Don't get me wrong," I assured the men, "we should absolutely take care of our customers. But not at the expense of our employees. It should always be both, never one or the other. That's why I have a two percent employee churn while most struggle to stay below twenty percent. That gives me the opportunity to pay them more because I don't need to retrain them." The sheepish looks on the faces of the men made it clear my point had landed. At the end of my lecture, the twenty-five business owners in that room formed a single file line, shook my hand, and promised me they were going to change the way they ran their companies.

Every single one of them.

People think I'm crazy for charging some of the highest prices in my area. But every year they see my smiling face on the A1 Garage Doors logo as our vans drive down their streets. We're growing nonstop. How are we still in business? People want to work for a company that Elevates its employees. Our customers are willing to pay more because we deliver an experience nobody else in the industry can match.

You can only support a team of A-players by charging high prices, and you can only do that if you deliver a superior product or service. The best employees have their pick of which company to work for. So why would they go somewhere with less support, fewer benefits, and lower pay? It's not realistic. Top people gravitate toward working for premium brands. They want to work with the best, most interesting, highest-paying customers. And those customers buy from top companies.

There is a famous idea in marketing known as the unattainable triangle. It has three sides: quality, speed, and price. The idea is that customers can be picky about two of these things, but not all three. Our product needs to either be cheap and fast, or high-quality and cheap, or fast and high-quality. So, companies have three options for how to provide their services. Except, an Elevated brand can't be cheap, so that eliminates two possibilities and only leaves us with one option: we must be fast *and* high-quality.

High profit allows a company to Elevate its people. Businesses that barely scrape by will have employees who struggle to survive. These companies must cut costs in a frantic race to the bottom, and in the end employees suffer. That's not right. Businesses should take care of our people. The way to do that is by taking extraordinary care of our customers too.

When you position your company as a premium service provider, this allows you to increase your margin so you can afford to support the five pillars from this book. Without taking this step, nothing else will work. And the only way to raise prices significantly is by improving the quality or speed of whatever you do.

When I talk to business owners about raising their prices, I get pushback. No, they assure me, that wouldn't work for them. It would scare away their customers, they tell me. It wouldn't be ethical to charge more, some say. Or else they mumble about how they kind of tried that before and it didn't work.

But that's the wrong way to think about it. The idea isn't to charge more for doing the same thing. You must offer more value in exchange for the higher price, that's how business works. When people do this the right way, it's never a challenge. They come back and thank me. I've done this with hundreds of entrepreneurs, and I've never had a single one come back and say it destroyed their business. The horror stories never come true.

Raise prices the right way. There is a process to follow. Don't suddenly charge 50 percent more. Work up to it.

Many other garage door companies in Phoenix hate me because I charge higher prices than nearly everyone else. Other business owners get angry with me sometimes, accusing me of ripping off customers because we charge so much. But they don't understand that to run an Elevated company you must charge higher rates.

Perspective matters a lot in pricing. I was recently furniture shopping, and I bought a nice couch for $2,600. Then I find out my friends bought a very similar looking couch for their house, but paid $30,000. They were happy with their purchase. That was their perspective because they saw the value!

I believe raising prices is one of the most important things most businesses can do to start the process of change. But remember that even before you raise your prices, you should first get your KPIs to work in your favor: your booking rate, your average ticket, your conversion rate and your cost per lead. Get those dialed in. Then, you make sure you get cost controls in place and a great controller. Finally, you build your price book based on the profit you want to make.

Look, I understand raising prices is not for everybody. This only works if you're ready to position yourself in the marketplace as a premium brand. If, for some reason you can't do that, or don't want to, this isn't the best decision for you.

* * *

The ideas in this book are for business owners who want to work with A-players. This approach is for people who want to serve good customers, rather than ones who complain and leave bad reviews about the stupid stuff. My book is for business owners who want to take proper care of their awesome employees. I have a hunch that's you since you've read this far. But, if not, sorry—this might not be your book.

As you implement the ideas from these pages, keep in mind that not everyone at your company has read this book and come to these conclusions in the same thoughtful and considerate way you have. They aren't necessarily going to understand why you're making these changes. To them, it could feel confusing to suddenly have so many aspects of the company shifting beneath their feet.

Keep people in the loop with what's going on. It's one of those things that is easy to do, but also easy to forget. I was on a flight once with the worst turbulence you can imagine. It felt like we were dropping floors at a time. The drinks flew into the air, the lights flickered, the lady next to me screamed, and I prayed (that's all you can do in a situation like that).

I gripped my armrest with white knuckles, waiting desperately for the pilot to come on and tell us what was happening. But he never made an announcement. He didn't say anything until at least ten minutes later.

"Sorry, folks," he finally said with a chuckle, "we got a bit of wind there." Well, I can tell you nobody in the cabin was chuckling, that's for sure.

Communicate. Let people know what you're doing, why you're doing it, when it's happening, and how they can get involved. I made a video every day during the first two weeks of COVID to let our people know we were working on everything and tell them not to worry.

Consistency is another big key to implementing the ideas from this book into your own business effectively. Don't wait to start hiring until you need somebody. That's too late. You can't look for good people part time. That's not how it works. Recruiting A-players is a full-time job that never sleeps. You've got to always be recruiting if you want to get any momentum.

Don't implement everything from this book tomorrow. Take things one step at a time. Go through the process every day. Another thing that stuck with me from a Simon Sinek Ted Talk is that you have to be consistent to see results. Think of it like this: one trip to the gym isn't going to produce any results in the mirror. But if you're consistent, after a few months the image will change, and you'll see remarkable results. The same applies to your business. You have to keep at it and not lose focus or faith that your efforts aren't working—they will if you are consistent.

You should know what the three to six main success metrics are for your business, and you should consistently check in on those. I have five main things I check up on every day during our motivational calls. Individual employees have their own success metrics on their scorecards, and we check in on those as frequently as possible too. Importantly, we check in on all five numbers all the time. We don't get too focused on one number or another specifically.

A couple years ago we realized we ended up cycling our focus around between the same five key numbers. So, we decided to formally commit to those five things and look at those each week instead of rotating our focus. That was a game-changing moment. We put everything together at the same time and found ways to consistently measure our progress in all five categories.

One of the most helpful things I've found for getting this all implemented properly is to maintain a schedule of regular one-on-one meetings with the key people throughout the transition. Figure out who the critical players are early on and get into the routine of meeting with them, ideally once per week, to talk about this project.

I currently do meetings at least once per month with the major people in my organization. And I've been working to get it happening every week instead. These meetings are that important to me. They are critical in any business, but especially in an A-player company.

As you implement the ideas from this book in your own company, take time to regularly pause and reflect on how things are going. It's a valuable practice. I'm trying to get better at pausing to assess myself, and that's been positive. Athletes look back and study tapes from last week's game. They reflect on their performance and make decisions about what they want to do differently in the next match.

Sometimes as companies grow there is a tendency for things to get overly complex, and we must fight for simplicity. Recently I added a new position called Maintenance Tech, and it is going to be a revolution in the industry.

"Guys," I told my team excitedly, "this is going to mean ten times the business! Here's why." Then people came up with these complications. I was quickly bogged down going through random wormholes. What was supposed to be simple became complex in the span of ninety seconds. I finally had to end the conversation.

"Stop," I said. "Please. At this rate you're going to push this out until 2092. It's not that hard. Don't make simple things overly complex. I told you the position, and I said how much I want to pay. I also told you what I want their responsibilities to be. You figure everything else out."

I'm frequently in the middle of complex situations because I'm always making tweaks to how things work at A1. And you should, too. Even after you implement everything from the book, your work is not done. Continue making changes to keep the company calibrated and on track.

At the same time, you don't want to let the implementation of these ideas drag on for too long. Get the full system up and running with all five pillars in place as quickly as possible. Then you can continue to tweak it from there. Some entrepreneurs fall into the trap of spending forever working on the pillars in isolation without ever getting them all implemented at once. Don't make that mistake. Get at least a basic version of all five pillars up and running, then refine it from there. Set a deadline for when you want implementation to be completed by, and enforce it.

I did this with my team by making a schedule of when we're going to start talking with private equity firms about selling the company. And that put everyone's focus into intense high gear. Can you find ways to create deadlines within your company, to motivate people to hit your goals by certain dates?

What's Your Turning Point?

Sometimes seeing how bad things could be motivates us to never let ourselves get to that point. When we know how deep the rabbit hole goes in a certain direction, we naturally avoid going anywhere near that area. Occasionally, a single event is enough to change the way someone relates to a topic forever.

I have a buddy, Aaron, who had a moment like that, where he suddenly saw what would happen if he didn't make changes in his life.

His son was four, and they were sleeping at Aaron's mom's apartment on the couch in the living room.

At that point, things hadn't been going well for Aaron during the past few years. He was in debt and struggling to find direction in his career. He was single, raising a child on his own. His social life was nonexistent. It felt like he was far behind, and he would never get ahead again.

Aaron looked down at his son and felt an overwhelming sense of shame. He was embarrassed to have a son but not a job or a place to sleep. He was embarrassed to be a dad when he didn't feel like a role model. This wasn't the life he wanted for himself or his young family.

"Chase," Aaron said, picking his kid up in his arms, "I promise you this is not going to be our life. I will not raise you like this. Your dad's better than this. You're never going to sleep on someone else's couch again."

That one glimpse down the rabbit hole was enough to scare Aaron out of failure. He realized what he didn't want and took responsibility for making sure things never got to that point. He went out and made a name for himself, and now he's a multi-millionaire. He put his kid through college, bought him a car, and they never slept on that couch again.

Aaron had to experience that night on the couch with his son in his mother's living room to see how bad things could get. That motivated him to finally change. Have you had your night on the couch yet in your business? Are you ready to do things differently?

There are many reasons business owners fail to get started, but one of the biggest is we decide what to do next based on our feelings, rather than relying on a non-biased analysis.

One example of how we can make basic judgment errors is a business owner who keeps getting sucked back into doing client work. Maybe a big project falls behind and the founder jumps in to pick up the slack and get it over the finish line. He gets to feel like a hero, his work generates a bump in revenue, the client is happy to have it done, and other employees are glad not to have to do the work themselves. It's a win-win-win.

Except, it's easy to fall into a dangerous pattern here. And this pattern reinforces itself. The entrepreneur does what feels best, not what's most helpful. There are a million things an entrepreneur could work on at any time. The behaviors we are familiar with are comfortable, but they are not likely the best actions to move the company forward. We do them all the time and yet we aren't where we want to be. So, to get to the next level, try something new. Spend time outside of your comfort zone.

Deep down, we know what we should do with our time. It's just like how we know we should eat salad and broccoli, but we still find ourselves gulping down a hot dog and a beer sometimes. Almost everyone has had the experience of trying to eat a strict diet for a while, but slipping up at some point, quitting, and going back to whatever was most comfortable and familiar.

Entrepreneurs often try to do the most helpful thing to grow our business. But when that doesn't work out quickly, and we experience rejection there, many of us quit and go back to doing what we are good at. Besides, the team could really use our help with a difficult client. Why don't we jump in and help them out on this one?

It makes us feel good as human beings to do things we are good at, and contribute positively to the common well-being. So, when we are beating our heads against the wall with boring stuff we know will help the company grow (but doesn't seem to be going anywhere), it's easy to quit and go back to putting out fires.

Another way it's easy to get pulled back into doing the wrong thing is if you have a need for the approval of others (and we all do). We are more likely to do things others will appreciate, even if there are more important tasks to take care of. For instance, it's hard to get excited about reading a new policy manual. So, when faced with an hour of reading new procedural updates, we might procrastinate by researching affordable gift baskets to send to our co-workers. Not to discourage this kind gesture, but it can't take the place of more important tasks.

Similarly, we also tend to be pulled toward behaviors that yield more immediate results, rather than long term ones. It feels better to get fast gratification for our efforts. Solving long term problems requires patience and faith, but it makes a bigger difference in the end. Putting in work on policies, structures, processes, and tech is like building a strong foundation for a building to stand on. It's like an old-timer sports coach who is always talking about "the fundamentals."

The final way our mindset can prevent us from taking the right actions to grow our business is when we know exactly what we need to do, but we talk ourselves out of even getting started. A good example of this is a policy manual. I've found you can tell a lot about the state of someone's business and their level of experience as an entrepreneur by asking to see their company's policy manual. Ironically, most small business owners don't have one.

"Yeah, I've thought about that," they often say. "But I never got started on it. I probably should do that soon." They have plenty of excuses about why they never got around to writing a policy manual. But at A1 we always had a policy manual, even from the beginning when we were a small company. Back then, it was just a few pages printed on regular paper. It was basic. But it always existed. I don't buy the excuses. We are so good at making excuses to ourselves for why we do certain things or don't do others.

Sometimes a better mindset is just to get started, even if you produce something imperfect. It's better to have something than nothing. You can always improve on it later. Just get started.

Doing What it Takes

Everyone knows that classic Dickens' story about Scrooge, a crabby old guy who experiences three key events in time and it changes his personality. I feel the same way about my own life. A few events have turned things around for me.

I hope reading this book can be one of those Scrooge moments for you too.

In *Spiderman* they say, "With great power comes great responsibility." And a similar thing is true is business: "We have the responsibility to grow at the rate we can grow." Everyone will navigate this differently.

Personally, I've got bigger huevos than most people. So, I'm willing to put it on the line with some calculated, aggressive moves. But you must decide for yourself how you will answer the question. How fast can you reasonably grow? That's how fast you should grow.

Of course, you can't predict the future, so it's impossible to say with certainty how fast you can grow one year, three years, or five years from now. But you can't throw up your hands and shrug your shoulders. Imagine a reporter asking the CEO where she sees the company in a couple of years, and she says, "I have no idea." That would not inspire confidence.

As the leader of the company, it's your job to have a vision, set goals, figure out the next moves, decide how fast you're going to grow, and tell people confidently what the game plan is. But at the same time, you can't stick too rigidly to the plan, because things change in the real world.

Yesterday, I was listening to a podcast and remembered this phrase: "You've got to let go if you want to grow." When you have the right checks and balances in place, and everyone is equipped for success, you can loosen your grip and take a step back. Once you Elevate your people, you can stop micromanaging them.

Back in the early days I ran this place with my buddy Adam and people called it the T&A Show because we were involved with everything. That was a hectic phase. Today, there are always a hundred things going on I'm unaware of. But it's all being done according to our procedures. And there are layers of checks and balances. So, I don't worry.

Figure out what you want, and then go get it. Your goals will change over the course of your life, and that's OK. Maybe right now you want to make $125k per year and spend your afternoons on the golf course. There's nothing wrong with that. Figure it out and go get it.

I used to dream of making $100 million, then we broke that. So, I had to come up with a new goal. Now I'm going for $10 billion. The real key is I love to win. However, don't base your goals on what I'm doing. Be honest with yourself about what feels right.

A friend texted me recently to say he's making $30k per month trading Tesla and I should be doing some of that on the side. I responded, "I don't try to guess that crap." See, what I know is if I hire the right people to work in my business, and put the right systems in place, with the right checks and balances, it's a certainty I will make money. That's not something I try to guess. It's guaranteed.

Other business owners sometimes look at me and say, "Wow, you do over a hundred million in revenue? You've arrived! You're killing it." But I have my sights set on $10 billion. Tommy is never satisfied. Heck, I haven't even started yet.

One thing I've learned as a leader is my dream has to be big enough for everyone at A1 to fit their own goals into mine. So, my dream needs to hold thousands of other dreams inside of it. In other words, your vision for the future of your company should represent a win for everyone who works there, not only for you.

A frustrating thing my friends, family, and co-workers notice about me is that I'm never satisfied. I want to pat everybody on the shoulder and say, "Great work, now it's time to get better."

One of my friends recently told me, "I love that you're never content." I was blown away. That guy gets me.

When you're making big changes in your business, the world can feel crazy and confusing. Pause and think to yourself before everything you do, "Does this bring me closer to my desired outcome?" Most of us have no idea what our desired outcome is, and that's a big part of the problem. We don't have dreams. We have vague goals, but nothing specific.

I recently found a line I'd scribbled in a journal many years ago, and it gave me chills.

Step out and design the life you want.

That means hire the right people, show them appreciation, and watch what happens. Find people who can take the ball and run with it. Stop being a slave to the business. And today that's all happening. We're getting the right people on the bus. Things are rolling faster every week.

It will happen for you too!

But don't try to do everything at once—focus on one thing at a time. When you lift weights, you can either build muscle or get ripped. It's difficult to do both simultaneously. You won't get as big if you're trying to stay ripped. You can add some muscle, but nothing significant. Similarly, you can't get shredded if you're too focused on not losing an ounce of muscle. Choose one main objective at a time.

A similar truth applies in the business world, where we can either work to grow our revenue (bulk up), or increase our profit margins (get ripped). But we can't do both simultaneously. There's no perfect combination, but choose a goal and stick at it.

I once sat next to pro golfer Xander Schauffele on a plane. All this guy did during the three-and-a-half-hour flight was watch videos of his golf swing on a laptop. It was hypnotic. He would bring the club back a few inches in slow motion and pause it for a while, then go back a few more inches. Then he watched his divots. He must have watched his swing hundreds of times during that one flight alone. And I had this realization: Oooh, that's what it takes to be one of the best in the world at something.

As you hire increasingly better people it raises the bar for what's possible in your company. At A1 we keep bumping up the numbers for what we expect in nearly every department, because our people and processes keep getting better. Constant improvement. That's how it should be. If you ever come across anyone who would be an amazing addition to the company, hire them immediately.

I do a call every couple of months where I specifically encourage people in my company to dream big. I say, "Remember when we were kids, how we used to think we were going to own the world? Well, I dare you to dream again. This is your chance. It's the chance of a lifetime. All you've gotta do is take it, right now."

As you start implementing the lessons from this book, you may find some resistance. That's normal. Change is not easy. Let me leave with you a few of my favorite thoughts to ponder.

1. "Do you know what hell on earth is? It's meeting what could

have been the best version of yourself—successful, fit, happy, and popular—only you never tried to get there. Don't put it off another minute. If you want to be the best in the world at something; if you want to help others become their best selves; if you want people to admire you for what you've accomplished; and if you want to feel calm and at peace because you've reached your true potential—now is the time to start."

2. "Don't take criticism from people you'd never go to for advice."

3. "Do you hate losing so much that you're willing to change? Or do you hate to change so much that you're willing to lose?"

4. "Excuses make today easy, but tomorrow harder. Discipline makes today hard, but tomorrow easier."

5. As I tell myself and my guys all the time, "Let's make sure we're the best version of ourselves today!"

Thank you for sticking with me to the end. To make it easier for you to implement everything I shared, I am giving away some of my best resources for you to use in your own business.

Just go to **https://tommymello.com/elevatebook**
or
email us at **elevatebook@tommymello.com**

About Tommy Mello

Tommy Mello is the owner and operator of A1 Garage Door Service, a leading $180+ million home service business based in Phoenix, Arizona, with over 700 employees in 19 states and 30 markets.

Originally from Detroit, Michigan, Mello moved to Phoenix in 1999 and began a career painting garage doors. Mello launched his business, which at the time was called A1 Garage Door Specialists, in 2007 while earning his master's degree in business from the University of Arizona. Overcoming several obstacles, he was able to shift from being $50k in debt to owning a multi-million home services company, currently the largest independently owned garage door company in North America.

In 2018, Mello wrote an Amazon best-selling book called Home Service Millionaire, which details his journey of going from $50,000 in debt to a $30 million business at the time. The book provides actionable advice for small business owners to immediately improve every aspect of their home service business. He also hosts a podcast called The Home Service Expert where he talks with leading entrepreneurs about the insights that have made them successful. Mello has appeared in several top publications and written for outlets such as Inc. and Entrepreneur.

Check in with us anytime. We are here to serve.

https://a1garage.com/

Bibliography

Eckstrom, Bill, and Sarah Wirth. *The Coaching Effect: What Great Leaders Do to Increase Sales, Enhance Performance, and Sustain Growth.* Greenleaf Book Group Press, 2019.

Frankl, Viktor E. *Man's Search for Meaning.* Beacon Press, 2006.

Lencioni, Patrick. *The Ideal Team Player: How to Recognize and Cultivate the Three Essential Virtues.* Jossey-Bass, 2016.

Levi, Al. *The 7-Power Contractor: Run Your Contracting Business with Less Stress and More Success.* Appleseed Business, Inc., 2016.

Miller, Donald. *Building a Storybrand: Clarify Your Message so Customers Will Listen.* HarperCollins Publishers, 2017.

Sinek, Simon. *The Infinite Game.* Portfolio Penguin, 2020.

Ingram Content Group UK Ltd.
Milton Keynes UK
UKHW051217050423
419604UK00025B/222

9 798885 810852